The Japanese Way

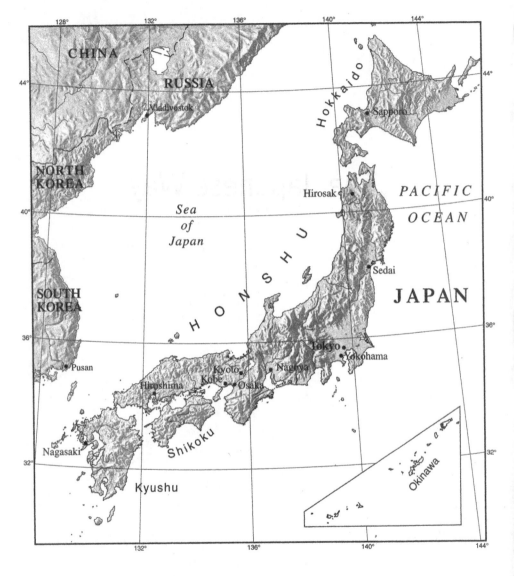

CHINA

RUSSIA

Vladivostok

NORTH
KOREA

Sea
of
Japan

SOUTH
KOREA

Pusan

Hokkaido

Sapporo

Hirosak

PACIFIC

OCEAN

Sedai

JAPAN

H O N S H U

Tokyo
Yokohama

Kyoto
Kobe   Nagoya
Hiroshima   Osaka

Shikoku

Nagasaki

Okinawa

Kyushu

0   100   200   300   400   500 Miles

0   100   200   300   400   500   600   700 Kilometres

The Japanese Way

Aspects of Behavior, Attitudes, and Customs of the Japanese

SECOND EDITION

Noriko Takada
and
Rita L. Lampkin

New York   Chicago   San Francisco   Lisbon   London   Madrid   Mexico City
Milan   New Delhi   San Juan   Seoul   Singapore   Sydney   Toronto

3 4 5 6 7 8 9 10 11 12 13 14 15 QVS/QVS 13

ISBN   978-0-07-173615-2
MHID   0-07-173615-8

Library of Congress Cataloging-in-Publication Data

Takada, Noriko.
        The Japanese way / Noriko Takada, Rita L. Lampkin. — 2nd ed.
            p.   cm.
        Includes bibliographical references and index.
        ISBN 978-0-07-173615-2 (alk. paper)
            1. Japan—Social life and customs.   2. National characteristics, Japanese.
        3. Japan—Handbooks, manuals, etc.   I. Lampkin, R. (Rita)   I. Title.

        DS821.T2347   2010
        952—dc22   2010016681

Map of Japan copyright © 1993 by Digital Wisdom, Inc.

McGraw-Hill books are available at special quantity discounts to use as premiums and sales promotions or for use in corporate training programs. To contact a representative, please e-mail us at bulksales@mcgraw-hill.com.

Bonus Audio Download

A bonus audio recording for this book can be obtained from mhprofessional.com. Simply follow these easy steps:

1. Go to mhprofessional.com.
2. Search for "The Japanese Way, Second Edition," or "9780071736152" (the book's ISBN).
3. Locate "Downloads" underneath the book's cover image.
4. Select link to listen and/or download.

This book is printed on acid-free paper.

CONTENTS

CONTENTS

INTRODUCTION

The first-time traveler to any foreign country—no matter what the person's place of origin and no matter how well he or she has prepared for the trip—is always surprised at the differences between expectations and reality. The greater the differences, the greater the surprise, and it is this surprise that constitutes what is called "culture shock," a potentially debilitating malady that can affect even the most enthusiastic visitor to the most paradisiacal locale.

It is not only the obvious differences that comprise the basis for culture shock, but the more subtle ones as well. Concepts that are taken for granted at home may be turned upside down in a different culture, and previously simple tasks—mailing a postcard, ordering dinner, hailing a cab, crossing the street—suddenly turn complicated.

Even experienced travelers within Western cultures are often amazed at the disparity between the habits, attitudes, and customs of the West and those of the various countries of Asia, where there are few—if any—shared roots. It is not uncommon for such a traveler to be overwhelmed by a feeling of helplessness and frustration as personal confidence and independence seem to fade into a sea of oddities. The person who only yesterday was praised for an ability in several European languages today arrives in Japan and struggles to remember the phrase for "Good morning." The young man who prided himself on being able to remember people's names and faces now complains that these homogeneous people "all look alike." The young mother who

INTRODUCTION

majored in English literature with a minor in Spanish now looks around her and cannot find so much as a billboard she can read.

Kipling's statement that "East is East, and West is West, and never the twain shall meet" has been cited as a discouragement and a warning to those who might venture too close to the "inscrutable Orient" without advance self-fortification, and it is this attitude that can actually create a predisposition to culture shock for travelers to Japan or other Asian areas.

The truth, however, is that it really takes only a modicum of preparation to dull the edge of culture shock; and if a person learns enough about what to expect of a country and its people, the visit is not only made more comfortable and enjoyable, but new and valuable insights and understanding can be brought home—souvenirs of more value than mementos from giftshops overseas.

To avoid culture shock—or at least to minimize it—it is necessary to know as much as possible about the country in advance of the trip. Studying the language of the country is helpful but may be insufficient in itself. There are many facets of culture unassociated with verbal communication, and often a study of the culture can help to make up for deficiencies in language ability.

This volume is intended and designed to guide the reader in gaining a basic understanding of the culture, customs, and attitudes of the Japanese, whether in preparation for a visit to Japan, in anticipation of visitors from that country, in an attempt to improve personal relationships with Japanese or Japanese-Americans, or simply to feed one's own curiosity about a fascinating people.

This offering is by no means represented as an exhaustive exposition of Japanese culture or any facet of it. Nor can the information herein be taken as a set of rules by which every single Japanese native lives. It may be said that there are as many different facets of any culture as there are people within that culture. Still, there are questions that are often asked about the Japanese that we have attempted to answer in this book, and we feel confident that what is presented in these pages can fill a great service by creating a hedge against culture shock and, at the same time, can make a small contribution toward the development of greater understanding and appreciation between East and West.

N.T. and R.L.

PRONUNCIATION AND ROMANIZATION

The Japanese language is fairly easy to pronounce. Unlike Chinese and some other Asian languages, Japanese has no "tones" that change the meaning of a word. It also does not have accented syllables like English and other Western languages.

There are only five vowel sounds in Japanese:

a as in "father"
i as in "machine"
u as in "tutu"
e as in "set"
o as in "hotel"

A macron (or "long mark") over a vowel indicates that the vowel is held for a longer time than a normal or "short" vowel. The length of a vowel can be crucial to the meaning of a word; for example, **obāsan** (grandmother) is actually five syllables(**o - ba - a - sa - n**), while **obasan** (aunt) is only four syllables in length (**o - ba - sa - n**).

Between unvoiced consonants (such as **k, p, t, s**), **i** and **u** are often silent or nearly silent; for example, **watakushi** (I, me) is usually pronounced as if there were no **u: wa - tak' - shi**.

Most Japanese consonants are similar to those in English, with the following exceptions:

r—Called a "single-tap r," this sound is made by tapping the tip of the tongue against the ridge behind the upper teeth, a little further back than when making a **d** or **t** sound. The **r** is similar to the **l**, but the tongue is not flattened. It is not rolled or trilled.

f—This sound, softer than an English **f**, is made by bringing the lower lip close to *but not touching* the upper teeth. The **f** sound is close to the **h** sound, but with a little more friction.

y—This soft consonant is always pronounced like the **y** in "you" and "yellow" and never as a separate vowel (such as the **y** in "lucky"). After a consonant it serves to palatalize or soften the consonant. The city name **Tōkyō**, for example, is often mispronounced by English speakers as "to-kee-yo."

n (or **n'**)—This sound is similar to the French **n** in **bonjour**. It never begins a word, and it maintains its soft, nasal quality when it comes before any vowel, but it hardens somewhat in front of most consonants. In front of **b, m,** or **p**, it sounds more like an **m**.

When a double consonant occurs in a word, both consonants are pronounced; for example, the word **suppai** (sour) sounds like "soup-pie."

Japanese expressions are presented in this book in the Roman alphabet (**rōmaji**). There are various systems of romanization in current use; the one used here follows that found in most romanized Japanese-English dictionaries currently published in Japan. For those who may be more familiar with other systems for transliterating Japanese into **rōmaji**, the following is a list of the major differences between the system used in *The Japanese Way* (TJW), and other common systems.

TJW	Others	TJW	Others
sha	sya	zu	du / dzu
shi	si	fu	hu
shu	syu	o	wo
sho	syo	nm	mm
ja	jya / zya / dya	nb	mb
ji	di / zi	np	mp
ju	jyu / zyu / dyu	ā	aa
jo	jyo / zyo / dyo	ū	uu
chi	ti	ē	ee
tsu	tu	ō	oo
tch	cch		

Also, an apostrophe is used to distinguish the single-syllable soft consonant **n** from the hard **n** of **na, ni, nu, ne, no,** and **nya, nyu, nyo**. For example, **hon'ya** has three syllables: **ho - n - ya**.

1. ABBREVIATIONS AND CONTRACTIONS

An abbreviation, as used in English, is a shortened form of a word or phrase, often only a letter or two and usually followed by a period, as in **A.M.** and **P.M.** for "ante meridiem" and "post meridiem," or as in **p.** for "page."

A contraction is a word or phrase shortened by omitting one or more of the sounds, such as **can't** for "cannot" and **I've** for "I have."

In Japanese the only true abbreviations used are those borrowed from other languages, particularly English. Commonly used abbreviations include those referred to in the first paragraph above, plus the following (among many others):

Abbreviation	Japanese pronunciation	English meaning
g	**guramu**	gram
k	**kiro**	kilogram
cm	**senchi**	centimeter
m	**mētoru**	meter
[3]F	**surii-efu**	[3rd] floor
WC	**daburyū-shii**	water closet, restroom
km/h	**jisoku***	kilometers per hour

Occasionally, as in this case, the Japanese use a native word to express a borrowed abbreviation.

Contractions are often used in daily speech, although they differ from the English concept in that they often consist of alteration or omission of consonants, as well as omission of vowel sounds. One very common example is **ja** for **dewa** (as in **ja mata** or **ja arimasen**). Another that is heard frequently is **n'desu** for **no desu**, a phrase added at the end of many statements either to indicate that the statement is a reason for something that is under discussion or simply to soften the sentence.

Many contractions are a product of localized dialects, such as **wakaran** or **wakarahen** for **wakarimasen** and **ohayō gozansu**, **ohayōsu**, or **ōsu** for **ohayō gozaimasu**.

In general, the shorter the word or phrase, the more casual and familiar the tone of the conversation. Abbreviated words and phrases are used frequently among friends and in informal situations. In polite or formal conversations, such as business discussions and discourse with strangers or superiors, or when talking before a group, the longer, more formal forms are used.

2. ADDRESSES AND STREET NAMES

It is unreasonable in Japan to hop into a taxi and expect to be taken to a private residence with an address only. House numbers are not assigned according to grid location or position on a particular street, as in the West. Instead, buildings are grouped in blocks and numbered according to when each was built. As a result, consecutive numbers may not be on adjacent buildings, and a map and directions may be required to find a specific address.

In addition, many of the winding streets are a maze to those unfamiliar with an area, and some streets in residential areas are wide enough for motor bikes and pedestrians only. Most streets are not named, except for a few in some of the larger metropolitan areas. With the exception of Kyoto—the 1100-year-old former capital city— and some areas, such as Nagoya, which have been built or extensively rebuilt since World War II, city planning has not been a high priority of local governments.

A traveler would be wise to ask for a map (**chizu**) or very specific directions before setting out to look for an address or, better yet, arrange to meet someone at an exit of a train station (**eki**) in the area. And since a station may have several exits (**deguchi**), remember to ask which one.

Some helpful phrases are:

Chizu o kaite kudasai. (Please draw me a map.)
Dono yō ni ikeba ii desu ka? (How do I get there?)
Eki de aimashō ka? (Shall we meet at the station?)

3. ARTS AND CRAFTS

Many Japanese arts and crafts are internationally known for their unique character and quality. Some of the more familiar are **ikebana** (flower arranging), **shodō** (calligraphy), **origami** (paper folding), **bonasi** (miniature gardens), and **cha-no-yu** (tea ceremony), all of which are done with distinctive Japanese flair and ritual. Some that are not as familiar to the international community are Japanese traditional music and dance, lacquerware, wood carving, ceramic arts, woodblock prints, scroll and screen painting, doll-making, and kite-making—all of which vary from region to region within Japan.

People who gain renown for their skills in these and other areas of the arts and crafts may be designated by the Japanese government as "national treasures" and given special recognition, similar to the designation of a "poet laureate" in the West.

Travelers interested in purchasing handicraft items may ask for the **kyōdo zaiku** or **kyōdo miyage** section of any large department store.

4. ASKING DIRECTIONS

At the Station City people are usually in a terrible rush. Since trains and buses are unbelievably punctual in Japan, commuters are anxious to make all connections with minimal waiting. Consequently, these people have little or no time to spare, and if a traveler tries to stop someone to ask directions, he or she may be waved off with an abrupt gesture. Every station, however, has an information and assistance window, called **Midori no Madoguchi** (Green Window), where the traveler may ask for directions. Another solution is to look for young people or students in uniform, who are often anxious to try out their English.

On City Streets Police boxes (**kōban**) are located near train stations and at major downtown intersections. Most are small but solid structures of brick or concrete and have a small red light over the entryway, so as to be seen from a distance.

Police (**keikan**) are very helpful and well informed, especially about shops and homes in their own district. They will also have a map of the area posted and can point out the address the visitor is looking for. They may not, however, have extensive English ability, so it is helpful to have the address written down in Japanese, if possible. (Hotel clerks do that for their guests routinely.)

5. BATHING AND BATHHOUSES

At Home Bathing is almost a ritual in Japan. The traditional "bathing order" is guest first, then the male members of the family, with the females bathing last. With the changing times, this traditional order is not always observed, but "guest first" remains as a rule of courtesy.

Bath time is usually before the evening meal or at bedtime. When the announcement is made that the bath is ready, the guest is expected to go first, although it is considered good manners to hesitate and offer to let someone else go ahead, saying **O-saki ni dōzo** (Please go ahead of me). Still, the guest will eventually accept the honor.

The bathroom (**furoba**) usually consists of two rooms—an anteroom large enough to change clothes in, and the room where the bathtub (**o-furo**) is located. The toilet is separate from the bathing area in most homes.

Since bathwater is not changed with each person, soaping, washing, and rinsing must take place first outside the tub. This is done by means of a small hand-held shower head (traditionally a ladle or bowl was used to scoop water from the tub and pour it over the body). Since the floor is tiled and equipped with a drain, the person can wet himself down and soap up outside the tub. The bather then must rinse off all the soap before sinking slowly into the very hot water (considerably hotter than most Westerners find comfortable) to soak and relax.

It is important to keep the tub water clean and free of suds, leaving soap and soapy washcloths or ladles elsewhere. It is also a matter of courtesy to economize on bathwater as you rinse, since others will be following you, and it is good manners after the bath to express gratitude to the host and hostess.

Young children often bathe together and with a parent or other relative. Sometimes close friends of the same sex will take baths together, chatting and scrubbing each other's backs. Bath time is looked on as a special and happy occasion, as well as a bonding experience for family members.

Bathhouses and Japanese Inns   There are local bathhouses for people who live in small apartments and others who do not have **o-furo** in their own homes. Today public bathing facilities segregate men and women, and each section has a pool-sized tub. Proper bathing procedure remains the same here as at home—wash and rinse before stepping into the hot water. Small stools and faucets or hand showers are provided, and soap, washcloths, and towels are available. Shoes are left at the entryway, and disrobing is done in an anteroom that may have lockers or other security for clothes and other personal belongings.

Giggling or ogling is considered ill-mannered behavior in bathhouses, and swimming is not allowed.

6. BODY LANGUAGE AND GESTURES

Body language often has more impact than the spoken word, and since there are some sharp differences between Western and Japanese gesturing practices, it is advisable to become familiar with at least the more common gestures, particularly if you are on business in Japan. Following are some signals that may be different from what Westerners are used to.

me	Point to your nose, not your chest.
money	Make a circle with the thumb and forefinger. (Like the American signal for "okay.")
Come here.	Turn the hand *palm down*, and wave the fingers. (The American way of crooking the index finger with the palm up is a demeaning signal for the same message.)
No, thanks.	The open hand is held vertically, fingers pointed upward. The hand is waved back and forth (as if swatting at a gnat).
Excuse me.	Similar to "No, thanks," but the hand is waved forward and back, accompanied by a nod of the head. Used, for example, when making one's way through a crowd.
the boss	A raised thumb, as if showing "thumbs up" in American symbolism.
Leave it to me.	Tap the chest lightly with the open palm.
crazy	A circling motion with the forefinger near the ear, sometimes followed by flicking the middle finger with the thumb.

Others A couple of gestures to be avoided in polite company are raising the little finger or pointing to it with the thumb of the same hand, or putting the thumb between the index and middle fingers, as such signals have obscene sexual connotations.

There are some gestures used particularly by men to indicate hesitation, embarrassment, dismay, or confusion: for example, inhaling air audibly through the teeth, scratching the back of the head, or hitting the forehead lightly with the open palm.

A nod of the head periodically while someone is listening to you indicates only that the person hears what you are saying, not that he or she necessarily agrees with you. This gesture is often accompanied by an audible acknowledgment, such as **Ee, ee,** (Yes, yes) or **Naruhodo** (I see *or* I should have known).

Crossing the legs or folding the arms are postures that traditionally manifest authority and power. Frowning while speaking also conveys a feeling of power. When these signals are used by a junior member of a business group or by a young person (under 40), they may be interpreted as a sign of defiance, lack of manners, or arrogance. Also, putting one's feet up on a desk, table, or another chair is not well accepted in Japan, and is taken as a sign of arrogance and poor manners.

Silence is considered by the Japanese to be an indication of thoughtfulness, wisdom, or deep appreciation for what is going on around a person. Closing one's eyes while listening to a speaker indicates concentration on what the speaker is saying and is not considered rude. (*See also* "Bowing.")

7. BORROWED WORDS AND ACRONYMS

Many Japanese corporations adopt names and logos that use words or acronyms borrowed from foreign languages. This practice improves recognition and visibility in the international business arena, and foreign words are perceived by the Japanese themselves as having a special zest and glitter. Political parties and government ministries also have adopted acronymic labels, and **LDP** (Liberal Democratic Party) and **MITI** (Ministry of International Trade and Industry) are better known by those initials than by the Japanese versions of their names.

Acronyms may be pronounced according to the letters used, such as **JTB** (Japan Travel Bureau—pronounced "Jay-Tee-Bee"), or read as a word, as with **JAL** (Japan Air Lines/**Nihon Kōkū**—pronounced "Jaru" by the Japanese and "Jal" by English speakers). Occasionally they may be pronounced according to the Japanese names, as with **ANA** (All-Nippon Airways) pronounced either "**ana**" or "**Zen Nikkū**").

Some companies create "foreign sounding" names that may or may not have a basis in Japanese; for example, *Casio* is taken from the name of the company's founder, Tadao Kashio; *Camry* is one of Toyota's "Crown" series cars, and the name is taken from the Japanese word **kanmuri**, meaning "crown"; *Panasonic* is the internationally familiar name for Matsushita (the founder) Denki (electric); and the Ishibashi family, whose name means "stone-bridge," founded the *Bridgestone* Tire Company.

Small businesses often carry English or other foreign names, even though they may not relate well to the type of business (like the beauty salon called "Repair Shop") and may sound odd to foreign speakers (like the bar named "Drink Happy"). Clothing, accessories, and other products are sometimes imprinted with foreign words and phrases, often apparently without research into what the words mean, and frequently with spelling or grammar errors that are sometimes funny, sometimes shocking, and sometimes just strange: towels imprinted with "Patty and Jimmy like to play skate"; T-shirts with obscene words; and stationery that says, "Love and friendship worm the heart."

New and borrowed words spread quickly in Japan via the mass media. Some disappear as quickly as they are created, but many find their way into the standard lexicon. It has been estimated that as much as a third of the vocabulary used in daily conversation in large metropolitan areas is borrowed from other languages, particularly English.

Many of these words are modified, and all are given Japanese pronunciation, making it sometimes difficult to recognize them, even for speakers of the language of origin. Here are some common examples borrowed from English:

New Word	Derivation/Meaning
masu-komi	mass communications
wā-puro	word processor
paso-kon	personal computer

poke-beru	**pocket bell**/personal pager
mai-kā	**my car**/personal vehicle (not company-owned)
naitā	**nighter**/night game (baseball)
seku-hara	**sex**ual **hara**ssment
pēpā-doraibā	**paper driver**/someone who has a license but does not have a car

8. BOWING

Bowing is a Japanese way of saying "hello," "goodbye," "thank you," and even "I'm sorry." The depth of the bow and how long the head is kept lowered depend on the relative status of the people involved, relative age, and relationship to one another.

Children grow up learning how to bow appropriately. Some major department stores take pride in training new clerks to bow correctly to customers. Among the Japanese, the protocol of bowing can be a complicated issue. Foreigners, however, are not expected to understand or conform to the custom of bowing, and the Japanese often yield to the more international custom of shaking hands (though a handshake is often accompanied by a slight bow as well).

9. BRAND NAMES AND BRAND-NAME GOODS (BURANDO-HIN)

Until the early 1960s traveling to Western countries was limited to the privileged few. From such travels, brand names such as Burberry, Louis Vuitton, Mont Blanc, Soringen, Wedgewood, Tiffany, Cartier, Waterford, and the like were introduced to Japan as standards of excellence. The historical Japanese trait of appreciating quality prompts even lower- and middle-class families to choose **burando-hin** over less expensive or generic items.

This characteristic carries over into both business and personal

9

life. For example, signing a multimillion dollar contract with anything but a quality, brand-name writing implement would not be considered acceptable protocol. Sports and hobbies, such as hiking, skiing, tennis, and photography, call for recognizable equipment, accessories, and clothing.

Gift-giving is another area where common goods will not do. A walk through the first floor of major department stores will give an idea of the particular brand names that are currently in vogue. (*See also* "Gifts.")

10. BUSINESS CARDS (*MEISHI*)

Business cards have a special significance in Japan. A card reflects the company that a person represents, as well as the employee's title and position. This information determines not only the relationship between the giver and receiver of a card, but also the social rituals to be observed, from seating order to the level of language used between the two. (*See* "Honorific Speech.")

Business cards are kept in cardholders, since a dog-eared, wrinkled, or soiled card would reflect poorly on both the bearer and the organization the person represents. When people meet for the first time in a business situation, a ritualistic exchange of cards takes place before any discussion. Each party carefully takes a card out of the cardholder and presents it to the other person, holding the card with both hands. (The card should never be flipped across the table or otherwise treated as anything less than a gift.) The card is also received with both hands, studied by the recipient, and complimentary comments might be made regarding the company, the person's title, or even the Chinese characters used for the person's name. The card may then be carefully placed in the receiver's wallet or pocket.

If the exchange takes place at the conference table among several parties, it is traditional to approach individuals according to seniority, rank, or importance, if that information is known. Participants at the conference may then place the cards discreetly on the table in front of them, laying the cards out according to the seating arrangement. This practice can help a person remember who's who in the meeting.

It is considered poor manners to show business cards to others like a collection of baseball cards. The card is seen as an extension of the person and so should remain appropriately private.

11. CALENDAR

Although it has become more and more common over the years to do business according to the Western calendar, the Japanese still frequently use their own imperial calendar, which is based on the ruling years of the reigning Emperor.

When the Emperor ascends the throne, he chooses a name by which he will be known after his death. For example, the Emperor Hirohito, who took the throne in 1926, chose the name **Shōwa**, meaning "bright peace." When he passed away in January of 1989, he became known as the Emperor Showa, and the period 1926 to 1988 is the Showa Era. His son, Crown Prince Akihito, upon his accession, chose the name *Heisei*, meaning "peaceful accomplishment" or "accomplishment of peace."

Imperial eras over the last century are as follows:

Heisei (1989 to present)
Shōwa (1926 to 1988)
Taishō (1912 to 1925)
Meiji (1868 to 1912)

The first year of any imperial era is called **Gannen**, meaning "base year" or "original year." Subsequent years are given numbers: 1990 was **Heisei 2**, 1991 was **Heisei 3**, and so forth.

Dates are written with the year first, then the month and day, whether the imperial calendar or the Western calendar is used: 95.12.08 (December 8, 1995) or 7.01.15. (Because imperial calendar dates are written in abbreviated form for the current era only, the latter date is clearly **Heisei 7**, January 15. Dates from earlier eras are not written in abbreviated form.)

The Japanese calendar week traditionally began with Monday and ended on Sunday, but most current calendars follow the American custom of Sunday through Saturday.

The table below lists recent years according to the Heisei and Showa imperial eras and the corresponding years on the Western calendar.

Heisei 8	= 1996	Showa 54	= 1979	Showa 36	= 1961	Showa 18	= 1943
Heisei 7	= 1995	Showa 53	= 1978	Showa 35	= 1960	Showa 17	= 1942
Heisei 6	= 1994	Showa 52	= 1977	Showa 34	= 1959	Showa 16	= 1941
Heisei 5	= 1993	Showa 51	= 1976	Showa 33	= 1958	Showa 15	= 1940
Heisei 4	= 1992	Showa 50	= 1975	Showa 32	= 1957	Showa 14	= 1939
Heisei 3	= 1991	Showa 49	= 1974	Showa 31	= 1956	Showa 13	= 1938
Heisei 2	= 1990	Showa 48	= 1973	Showa 30	= 1955	Showa 12	= 1937
Heisei 1	= 1989	Showa 47	= 1972	Showa 29	= 1954	Showa 11	= 1936
		Showa 46	= 1971	Showa 28	= 1953	Showa 10	= 1935
Showa 63	= 1988	Showa 45	= 1970	Showa 27	= 1952	Showa 9	= 1934
Showa 62	= 1987	Showa 44	= 1969	Showa 26	= 1951	Showa 8	= 1933
Showa 61	= 1986	Showa 43	= 1968	Showa 25	= 1950	Showa 7	= 1932
Showa 60	= 1985	Showa 42	= 1967	Showa 24	= 1949	Showa 6	= 1931
Showa 59	= 1984	Showa 41	= 1966	Showa 23	= 1948	Showa 5	= 1930
Showa 58	= 1983	Showa 40	= 1965	Showa 22	= 1947	Showa 4	= 1929
Showa 57	= 1982	Showa 39	= 1964	Showa 21	= 1946	Showa 3	= 1928
Showa 56	= 1981	Showa 38	= 1963	Showa 20	= 1945	Showa 2	= 1927
Showa 55	= 1980	Showa 37	= 1962	Showa 19	= 1944	Showa 1	= 1926

12. CHERRY BLOSSOMS AND FLOWER VIEWING

The **sakura**, or cherry blossom, has been held dear by the Japanese through the centuries, both personally and in poetry, literature, and other art forms.

The nonbearing, flowering cherry tree is unique to Japan. In the spring TV viewers can follow the "Sakura Front Line" on the weather map as flowers begin blossoming in Okinawa, the southernmost island, and slowly make their way northeast through the main island of Honshu, until they finally begin blooming in Hokkaido in the north.

During the short, two-week flowering season, social conversation turns to **sakura**. People make travel plans to go flower viewing or take food and drinks to local parks and gardens to picnic among the beautiful blossoms. Traditionally, this was also a time for contemplation, personal reflection, and even the composition of original poetry.

13. COMPLIMENTS

Although compliments may flow naturally among family members and friends in a casual situation, in more formal settings compliments received for oneself or family members are carefully downgraded. A person who accepts compliments too readily may be considered conceited or lacking in good manners. The expected response is first to deny the compliment (**Iie, iie, sonna koto wa arimasen**—No, no, that's not true), and then to express gratitude for the thought (**Dōmo arigatō gozaimasu**—Thank you very much).

The Japanese will emphatically deny any compliment made in reference to themselves, their children or anything that pertains to them, and then they will negate the compliment by pointing out some fault or weakness in the person complimented. For example, if a teacher reports to a mother that her daughter is a good student, the girl's mother may respond with, "Yes, but she argues with her brother at home all the time" or "Thank you very much, but I can't get her to keep her room clean."

Although compliments are given generously to a person for accomplishments (passing entrance exams, graduation, marriage, promotions, a foreigner's Japanese speaking ability, and so forth), most Japanese do not make a point of complimenting a person on dress or appearance. When someone does make such a compliment on, for example, a piece of jewelry, it is not unusual for the Japanese person to make a present of the item to the person who paid the compliment.

14. CONVERSATION

One very typical Japanese characteristic during conversation is for the listener to insert commentary words or phrases as the other person speaks. This continual commentary is carried on whether the conversation is in Japanese or in English, and it can be distracting to the foreigner who is not familiar with it. The practice is called **aizuchi** and ranges from **Ee, ee** (Yes, yes), **Naruhodo** (I see/Of course), **Hontō desu ka?** (Really?) to interjected expressions of agreement, **Sō desu, ne. Subarashikatta desu, ne** (Yes, it was wonderful, wasn't it?), to chiming in to help the speaker complete a sentence. When more than two people are involved, one of the listeners may solicit agreement from the others: **O-tenki wa hontō ni warukatta desu, ne?** (The weather really was bad, wasn't it?).

Also part of **aizuchi** is a constant nodding of the head by the listener, signifying that he is listening intently. This is often mistaken by foreigners as a sign of agreement or encouragement to continue talking, but to the Japanese it has no such connotation.

The word **aizuchi** originates in the practice of two people standing opposite each other, hammering a stake into the ground and signaling to each other as they do so, so that they do not miss a stroke.

Other characteristics of Japanese conversational style include the following:

Request for Confirmation Tag questions (. . ., ne? / . . ., deshō? / Sō ja arimasen ka?) are far more frequent in Japanese conversation than in English. This practice conforms with the tradition of maintaining a humble public image. Also, when confirmation is given, it is likely that the Japanese person will express agreement with at least a part of what has been said, before making any contradictory statement, no matter how positive the person may be about it. For example, the comment **Ii tenki desu, ne?** (The weather is beautiful, isn't it?) may elicit a different response from a Japanese than from a Westerner.

Westerner: Yes, but I hear it's going to rain tomorrow.

Japanese: **Sō desu, ne. Hontō ni ii o-tenki desue, ne? Demo . . . ashita ame ga furu sō desu yo.** Yes, it really

is a fine day, isn't it? But . . . (after some hesitation)
I hear it is going to rain tomorrow, you know.

Small Talk   It is common for persons in America and other Western countries to add considerable miscellaneous "small talk" when greeting one another. For example, rather than just saying "Hello," we might add, "How are you?" or "How's your family?" The Japanese, however, usually stick to a simple greeting and a bow or nod. Also the Western custom of including a person's name in a greeting ("Hi, John." / "How are you Mrs. McGinnis?") is not considered essential to the Japanese.

Silence   Silent moments do not make Japanese people feel uncomfortable. When a conversation comes to an end, a person may savor the silent moment to think about what has been said. Business people often utilize pauses and silent moments to rethink their strategy. (*See also* Body Language and Gestures.)

15. CRIME AND SAFETY

Despite occasional problems with radical individuals or militant groups, as well as the internationally notorious, Mafia-like **Yakuza** crime organization, the relatively low crime rate, even in large metropolitan areas, makes Japan an attractive place to visit.

There is a strictly enforced ban on handguns, although police officers always carry a gun while on duty. To have a gun for sports and competition purposes, a person must apply for a permit and receive gun training at the same time. Hunting specific game animals is permitted during specified seasons, and permits are required.

The Japanese generally have a high regard for personal property, and "finders, keepers" is not the normal rule. Lost personal items often turn up at the lost-and-found office (**ishitsubutsu toriatsukaijo**) at the local police box (**kōban**), or even in the places where they were left.

Of course, foreigners stand out in this highly homogeneous society, and tourists often find themselves being stared at, singled out, approached by people who want to try out their English, or called to by friendly drunks. Most of this behavior is totally harmless; still, it is a good idea to exercise due caution in watching out for your personal safety and belongings, even in the safest countries.

Foreigners who are in Japan for any length of time may want to check in at the nearest police box, and tourists should also familiarize themselves with the location of the embassy of their own country.

16. DATING AND MARRIAGE

Couple dating has become more and more frequent in Japan over the last 20 or 30 years, although courtship usually begins considerably later than is typical in the West. Boys and girls of junior high and high school age are rarely seen openly pairing off, dating, or going steady, and couples wait longer to get married than do their Western counterparts. Dating itself is not as frequently practiced as it is in the West, and group activities are more common than couple dating.

At universities and other institutions, there are extracurricular activities called **bukatsu** (club activities) that are based on sports, academics, or hobbies, and these are strongly supported by students and faculty alike. Nearly all students belong to one or two of these clubs, where they continue to develop a sense of group identity, which is often maintained through later married life.

A Japanese marriage ceremony (**kekkon shiki** or **uedingu**) is a very expensive ritual, often running well into six figures (in yen) even for simple ceremonies, and costs are shared by the families of both the bride and the groom. The couple may choose a traditional wedding, where all involved parties wear **kimono** and participate in Shinto ceremonial rites, or—a growing trend in recent years—Christian-style nuptials, including wedding gown and tuxedo for the happy couple and an elaborate postvow celebration around an ostentatious wedding cake.

Whether the wedding is traditional or Westernized, a honeymoon (**hanimūn**) abroad has become a popular goal. The number-one choice for recent couples has been Hawaii, with Guam and other Pacific islands also considered respectable destinations.

Appropriate dress for a foreigner attending a wedding is Western formal wear. (*See* "Dress.") Some words and phrases that may be helpful at a wedding include the following:

shinrō / hana mukō-san groom

shinpu / hana yome-san bride

Hanimūn, doko e ikimasu ka? Where are you going on your honeymoon?

subarashii kappuru wonderful couple

Often guests are asked to make an impromptu congratulatory speech. In such a case it is best to make a *short* speech in English without hesitation, perhaps ending with **O-medetō gozaimasu** (Congratulations).

17. DEATH, FUNERALS, AND MOURNING

Funerals are solemn, reverent occasions in Japan, and bereaved families and friends of the deceased take comfort in Shinto and Buddhist teachings of an afterlife. For the most part, the preparation process for burial involves cremation. Burial grounds contain stone monuments or wooden plaques commemorating the deceased. A family may have its own cemetery or section of a cemetery. A number of historical figures are memorialized in more elaborate ways, such as the grand shrine at Nikko, called **Tōshōgū**, where the shogun **Tokugawa Ieyasu** (1542 to 1616) is buried.

It is also customary to give a gift of money to the family of the deceased, consisting of unused, uncreased bills presented in a special funeray envelope (**sōgiyō noshibukuro**), which can be purchased at department stores and stationery stores (**bunbōguya**). These envelopes come in three religious styles: Buddhist (**okōden**), Shinto (**go-**

reizen), and Christian (**ohanadai**). As an alternative, a sheet of white stationery may be folded around the bills and the whole inserted into a plain white envelope.

A wake is usually held at the family home, where the entryway is draped with black-and-white curtains. Mourners are guided to the home from the main street by black-bordered sheets of paper displaying the family name, posted on lamp posts along the route. Some Buddhist and Shinto believers hold funeral services at home, and others utilize a local church or rented hall.

Death notices—postcards with black borders—are sent to friends and acquaintances. When visiting a home following a funeral, it is appropriate to take white cut flowers to honor the deceased. Mourning periods and other traditions vary according to religion and family custom.

18. DIALECTS

There are numerous local dialects throughout Japan, but people from all areas, including Okinawa, can communicate with one other in the standard dialect (**hyōjun-go**), which has evolved from the speech patterns used by people in the Tokyo area over the centuries.

The Japan Broadcasting Association (**Nihon Hōsō Kyōkai** or NHK) trains and requires its broadcasters to speak **hyōjun-go** and has published an extensive guide, **Akusento Jiten** (Accent Dictionary), that outlines appropriate pronunciation and intonation. With the advancement of mass media, even those in the remotest areas of Japan are exposed to standard speech patterns. It is also taught in the schools as **gakkō yōgo** (school language), enabling children to become proficient from an early age.

Speaking **hōgen** (nonstandard dialects) or **chihō no kotoba** (rural dialects) is considered by some to be unsophisticated, despite recent efforts at decentralization, and most people avoid the use of nonstandard speech when talking with people from outside their own area.

The one exception to this is those who speak **Kansai-ben** (the dialect spoken in the Kobe, Osaka, and Kyoto areas).

19. DINING OUT

Trying out various places to eat in Japan can be an enjoyable experience. An excellent place for a first venture out is a department-store restaurant section. An entire floor, usually the top, houses a variety of eating places from restaurants to fast-food take-out stands. A quick walk through the entire floor will show you what is available, usually a broad variety of both Oriental and Western foods.

Another good place to find a variety of foods is the **chikadō** (underground street) built in conjunction with major subway stations in a number of large metropolitan areas (Tokyo, Osaka, and Nagoya, in particular). These areas are well lighted and pleasant; and the food is generally of high quality.

Every **resutoran** (restaurant) and **shokudō** (eating place) has an outdoor display cabinet containing **shokuhin sanpuru** (life-size plastic replicas of dishes on the menu) with the price of each item clearly posted. If you are uncertain about ordering in Japanese, it is acceptable to bring the waiter or waitress outside and point to the replica of what you want to eat. (In most cases, the plastic replica is a very close duplicate of what you actually get, down to the number of slices and size of portions.)

Noren   Hanging over the entrances of many restaurants, particularly traditional Japanese and Chinese establishments, are short curtains made of four or five panels with slits in between. These **noren** carry the name of the establishment and are designed and colored according to the specialty served within. A dark blue **noren** with white writing indicates a **sobaya** (noodle shop), **sushiya** (sushi restaurant), or **unagiya** (eel specialty shop). A white **noren** with red writing shows that **chūka-ryōri** (Chinese food) is served.

It is normal procedure to push one section of the **noren** aside with the back of the hand and enter the restaurant upright, rather than stooping to walk under it; however, tall foreigners should take care not to collide with the door frame overhead, since doorways are not built as high as the Western standard.

Aiseki   Some larger restaurants, particularly those that specialize in foreign foods, will have a host or hostess stationed near the entrance to seat customers. In more traditional restaurants, however, the customer is expected to find his or her own table. During busy hours it may be necessary to share a table with strangers. This system is called **aiseki**. Conversation with strangers at the table is not required, although it is a matter of normal courtesy to say **Shitsurei shimasu** (Excuse me) when sitting down at a table that is already occupied.

O-shibori   Although napkins are not always available in a Japanese-style restaurant, it is common for the waitress to bring **o-shibori** for each customer. The **o-shibori** is a damp (often hot, especially in cold weather) hand towel used to wash the hands before eating. (Although some people, in very casual surroundings, may wash the face and neck with it also, it is not considered the best manners.) **O-shibori** may come individually packaged in plastic, and they are usually served on a small tray. They are often kept in large quantities in a temperature-controlled container until served.

Kōhii Shoppu (coffee shops) and **Kissaten**   For breakfast or a light snack during the day, a variety of small shops can be found along any busy metropolitan street. During the morning hours, you can enjoy **mōningu sābisu** (morning service)—typically a cup of coffee and a piece of very thick, buttered toast with jam—at a reasonable price. The coffee is quite strong and there are no free refills. Also, you should be aware that any imported fruit, including most citrus and melons, are extremely expensive in Japan. **Mikan** (mandarin oranges) are grown locally and are a less expensive way to satisfy a taste for citrus fruit. They are sweet, tasty, easy to eat, and packed with Vitamin C.

Kissaten (coffeehouses) are common in Japan, although the coffee is expensive, and again there is no free refill. The high price includes the ambience and the opportunity to relax and enjoy. Coffee drinking has become a matter of fashion in Japan, and many people are very particular about the blends they drink. If you ask for **Amerikan**, the cup is larger, and the brew is not as strong. Sometimes waitresses refer to a cup of hot coffee as **hotto kōhii** (hot coffee). **Aisu kōhii** (iced coffee) is popular and very refreshing in hot weather.

Fast Food The idea of eating on the run is not totally foreign to Japanese tradition, since sidewalk vendors were part of the Japanese scene as early as the 1700s, when itinerant merchants peddled noodles from portable stands. The Western concept of "fast food," however, was not introduced until 1970, when Colonel Sanders' Kentucky Fried Chicken booth became a major success at the World's Fair in Osaka. The company set up a permanent KFC restaurant in Nagoya later that year, becoming the first foreign food chain established in Japan.

An A&W franchise setup in Kobe did not see the same positive results because the Japanese had difficulty developing a taste for root beer. However, other companies had greater success over the next two decades, including the phenomenal popularity of McDonald's, which started with one walk-in restaurant in Tokyo in 1971 and by 1993 had established 1,100 stores nationwide, serving nearly 6.5 million customers in that year alone.

Pizza was a little slower to catch hold, until the toppings had been adapted to suit the Japanese palate: less cheese and more seafood. Shakey's and Pizza Hut now compete with Domino's, which introduced the guaranteed 30-minute delivery. Taco Bell and El Pollo Loco have also prospered.

For all of the foreign-based enterprises, store setups and decor, uniforms, and menus (with some variation) are the same as they are in the country of origin, but food names are pronounced the Japanese way: coffee is **kōhii**, hamburger is **hanbāgā**, and dark meat is **dāku**. Franchise names have also been Japanized, as in the following names for some of the most popular chains:

Makku (McDonald's)
Kenta (Kentucky Fried Chicken)
Ābiizu (Arby's)
Uendiizu (Wendy's)
Dankin Dōnattsu (Dunkin' Donuts)
Mistā Dōnattsu (Mister Donut)
Sheikiizu (Shakey's)
Pisa Hatto (Pizza Hut)
Dominōzu (Domino's)
Takoberu (Taco Bell)

20. DINNER INVITATIONS

The Japanese usually prefer to entertain guests at restaurants rather than at home—with the exception of family gatherings, particularly during holidays—and these occasions are often catered. There is, however, a current trend among younger couples without children toward sharing a meal at home. It is also popular to invite foreign guests to the home, and after a dinner party at a restaurant, guests are sometimes invited to the home for drinks and conversation. Women and children sometimes get together for lunch, and men often meet with colleagues for drinks or dinner after work. (*See* "Drinking.")

When accepting an invitation to have dinner at a restaurant, it is not necessary to bring a gift, unless the occasion specifically warrants it, such as when it is the last time the parties will see one another. Neither is a gift expected when guests are invited to the home following a dinner out, although someone in the party may order a take-out (sushi, for example) for the lady of the house, if she was not at the dinner party. Normally, however, guests will come **tebura** (without a gift). Sometimes, also, a reciprocal invitation is extended to the host.

When a dinner invitation is business related, spouses are not normally invited. If a foreign businessman brings his wife on a trip, however, the invitation may be extended to her, as well. In such cases the Japanese host will bring his wife, also. When a man invites a guest home for drinks after dinner, it is normally after having given his wife fair warning, so that she has time to shop and prepare.

After having been treated to drinks or dinner, an expression of appreciation should be included when greeting the host the following day or on the first subsequent meeting. Commonly used phrases are **Kinō wa dōmo** or **Senjitsu wa dōmo** (Thank you for yesterday/the other day.) Failure to do so would be considered both rude and ungrateful.

21. DIRECTNESS

Openness and a direct, straightforward manner are considered admirable traits in the West; however, the Japanese tradition is very different. Although basic honesty is admired, aggressive self-assertiveness is not part of the Japanese culture and is generally considered to be offensive. This principle is reflected in the language, where **to omoimasu** (I think) is added to any sentence that expresses an opinion and to many statements that convey facts, even when the speaker is quite certain about what he is saying. For example, the following exchange occurred in an American court, when a Japanese defendant was responding through an interpreter:

Attorney: What color was the traffic signal?
Defendant: I think it was green. (**Guriin datta** *to omoimasu*.)
Attorney: You think? You are not sure?
Defendant: No, I am sure it was green, *I think*. (**Iie, tashika ni guriin datta** *to omoimasu*.)

One habit of the Japanese that is difficult for many Westerners to deal with—particularly those doing business with the Japanese—is the avoidance of "no." A flat refusal to do something or an admission of the impossibility or unfeasibility of a request is replaced by a response that sounds to foreign ears as a hopeful possibility. A common refusal is expressed by **Muzukashii desu** (It's difficult), which really means "It's impossible," "It's not going to happen," or "I don't want to do it."

In accordance with this tendency to avoid confrontation, gifts are accepted only after much hesitation, and compliments to oneself or one's family are vigorously denied. Direct, pointed, or personal questions are also avoided, and public display of affection is looked down on. Getting right to the point in a conversation or speaking one's mind in a direct manner can be interpreted as rude, arrogant, and inconsiderate. Even in business correspondence, the Japanese will often refer first to the weather or some other pleasantry before getting down to business.

Another manifestation of this trait is the Japanese custom of smiling when a situation is difficult or disagreeable, which stems from a desire to avoid confrontation or embarrassment, and should not be construed as an indication of either pleasure and agreement or patronizing contempt.

22. DISCUSSION AND CONSENSUS

There are unspoken rules observed by the Japanese as they discuss either business or social matters, but the key is "consensus building."

In Japanese dialogue, coming directly to the point or speaking out with too much confidence can be interpreted as brash or rude and a sign of the speaker's inability to recognize his or her own limitations. A centuries-old proverb says, **Deru kugi wa utareru** (The nail that sticks up will be pounded down).

As an example, at a business meeting when Delegation A brings a proposal to Company B, members of B will listen intently, take notes, nod heads, and make general comments ("I see," "I understand," and "You've done a great deal of preparation,") and so on. The meeting will then come to an end when the senior official of B promises a response "soon." Company B will subsequently hold a reviewing session with experts from all sections present, and with everyone participating actively in the discussion. Out of a meeting like this, consensus is reached and a counterproposal emerges. It is practically unheard of for a first meeting to end with a signed contract or even a handshake agreement.

When a presentation is being made, the Japanese businessperson will never interrupt the presenter, no matter how sincerely the presenter may invite questions. This is especially true if the presentation is made in the Western tradition—polished, enthusiastic, concise, and backed with all the necessary facts and figures. By comparison, the Japanese presenter will avoid the appearance of flaunting his knowledge or having all the answers, gearing his speech to allow for (and even require) questions and comments from his audience. He will speak relatively slowly and pause between major points.

23. DRESS

In general the Japanese dress fairly conservatively in public. Sundresses, shorts, tanktops, jeans, sleeveless outfits, flashy prints, splashes of colors are considered resort wear and are not worn in cities or on domestic sightseeing tours.

Standard business attire is suit-and-tie for men and subdued colors and styles for both men and women. Ōeru (from "O.L." for "office lady," referring to female clerical staff) often wear uniform dresses or smocks. Women office employees do not wear slacks unless their work requires it, and pantsuits are seen only in businesses that call for a more liberal or "progressive" image (entertainment or designing, for instance).

Public junior high and high school students usually wear school uniforms, although a number of schools are currently moving away from that practice. Younger students do not wear uniforms, except for regulation brightly colored (usually yellow) headgear for traffic safety reasons.

Private school students proudly wear school uniforms. Some schools have regulation coat, scarf, and schoolbag as well. A strict dress code may include hairstyle and length of skirt.

Weddings and funerals are extremely formal and ceremonious. Even when an event is declared to be "casual," it is advisable to ask others what they will be wearing. For weddings, women usually wear cocktail dresses, and men wear dark suits and ties. Funerals call for traditional funeral kimono, although of course, foreigners are expected to dress according to their own customs (that is, suit-and-tie). Black is the accepted color for all clothing for a funeral, including accessories. Patent leather and other shiny materials are also considered inappropriate. Even buttons may be covered temporarily with special black button covers sold for the purpose. Jewelry is minimal—usually plain pearls—and nail polish is not worn.

24. DRINKING

The legal drinking age in Japan is 20. Underage drinking is not considered a major problem, even though alcoholic beverages are readily available from public vending machines, which often carry a variety of drinks, including cold beer and hot or cold **sake** (rice wine). Local products are reasonably priced, but imported liquor is very expensive.

For the Japanese **sarariiman** (white-collar worker), it is considered obligatory to go out drinking with coworkers after hours on a fairly regular basis. Nondrinkers are rare in Japan, and even women will sometimes join a mixed or all-female group for a drinking party. Common phrases of invitation and acceptance include the following:

Biiru demo dō desu ka? How about a beer or something?

Ii desu ne. Ikimashō. Sounds good. Let's go.

Sumimasen. Kyō wa, chotto. . . Sorry. I can't make it today.

When drinking with friends, it is polite to allow a friend to pour your drink for you, then you quickly fill your friend's glass. When drinking **sake** (also called **Nihon-shu**—Japanese wine), a tiny cup is used, called an **o-choko**. When you have sipped from your drink, your glass will be filled again. To signal that you have had enough, either turn your empty glass or **o-choko** upside down or simply stop drinking.

25. DRIVING

The Japanese drive on the left side of the roadway; vehicles are all right-hand drive, as in Great Britain. Even in large metropolitan areas, most surface streets are narrow and congested, and rush hours bring horrendous traffic jams. For a foreigner especially, driving a car under these conditions can be hectic at best and even dangerous for the inexperienced. Most foreigners (along with a large majority of Japanese as well) opt for the convenience of mass transit for local travel. However, an international driving license can be obtained through your local automobile club before leaving home. Be aware, however, that most of the road signs, especially in rural areas, are written only in Japanese script.

Parking is limited in all downtown areas in major cities and their suburbs, and a car cannot be registered unless the new owner can show proof that he has a place to park it. Automobile manufacturers and dealers now offer assistance in locating parking space for potential customers. A two-car family with space for only one car may have to erect a system where the two cars can be stacked vertically.

26. EARTHQUAKES

Seismic activity is as common in Japan as in California. The Tokyo area has not experienced a major quake since the Great Earthquake of September 1, 1923; however, the Hanshin (Osaka and Kobe) area was hit by a 7.2 (Richter scale) quake on January 17, 1995, causing extensive damage, particularly in the vicinity of Kobe.

Earthquake-resistant architectural design research was pioneered in Japan, and all new construction, including residential buildings, is subject to a specific earthquake code. There are, however, many older structures that are more susceptible to damage from an earthquake. And of course, when the jolt is as severe as the Hanshin quake, even buildings that are up to code are not immune to damage.

27. EDUCATION

As early as the Japanese feudal period (roughly 1600–1858), schools of various types were in operation in Japan. Regional lords (**dai-myō**) provided education for the offspring of the warrior class (*See* "Social Structure."), and local communities established learning centers to teach reading, writing, and arithmetic for children of commoners.

During the Meiji Period (1868–1912), the government established the national educational system (1872), and the Compulsory Education Act was passed in 1876, requiring three to four years of school for all children. In subsequent years this system evolved into two tracks: the eight-year trade track and the academic track, which provided for six years of elementary school, five years of middle school, and two years of high school, plus four years of college. The present "6-3-3" system was introduced during the Allied Occupation following World War II, and a total of nine years of education became compulsory. Today, the drop-out rate is low, and most Japanese children complete the additional three years of high school. Over 40 percent of high school graduates pursue higher education, and the literacy level in Japan is over 99 percent.

By grade five, the majority of elementary school children have been enrolled by their parents in after-school tutoring classes, collectively called **juku**. Core subjects include language arts, social studies, math, science, English, calligraphy, and abacus. One specialty of **juku** is test preparation for junior high and high school entrance exams, concentrating not only on specific subject matter but on test-taking skills as well.

Graduation from a prestigious university (public or private) is believed to be necessary for career success. Children are, therefore, subjected to fierce educational competition from an early age. Entrance into a school essentially assures graduation; however, rigorous entrance examinations are required, and the more prestigious the school, the more competition there is for acceptance. Private schools that offer kindergarten-through-university programs are vigorously sought by parents with hopes of shielding their children from the grueling exams. Failing that, the student must spend many hours preparing for the exams, an experience known as **shiken jigoku** (examination hell), including after-school tutoring classes (**juku**), as well as many hours of solitary study, while the student's family caters to needs for physical sustenance and an atmosphere conducive to concentration.

Some prestigious universities accept students at a ratio of one out of every 15 applicants, based on stiff entrance exams. Since not every student will be accepted into the school of choice, many students wait a year and retake the exam a second or third time. In the meantime, they try to strengthen their abilities in key subjects by taking classes in specialized college-entrance preparatory schools, called **yobikō**.

This major emphasis on educational prestige has not been without negative consequences and has become a serious social issue in recent years.

28. ENGLISH-LANGUAGE STUDY

Although English is one of the core subjects in junior and senior high schools in Japan, the "textbook" approach gives little or no actual practice in oral communication. As a result, after six years of study, few high school graduates actually speak English. They do, however, gain a fairly extensive vocabulary and are often able to understand the written word to some extent.

Many adults enroll in **eikaiwa** (English conversation) classes to improve their speaking ability for career, travel, or personal purposes. Such classes are offered by private companies or schools that specialize in foreign-language or specifically English-language instruction. Many large Japanese businesses offer English instruction as either a benefit for employees or as preparation for overseas assignment.

29. FAMILY

Although the Japanese have a high regard for children and historically had large families, currently most families have no more than two or three children. This is the result of post-World War II social policy designed to relieve the problems caused by severe food shortages, lack of housing in some areas due to wartime bombing, the influx of expatriates, and other factors.

The increase in personal mobility in recent decades has resulted in the weakening of the centuries-old Japanese concept of the extended family. There is still, however, a strong obligation to fulfill certain traditional responsibilities, particularly those that fall to the eldest son.

As the parents age and become less able to function as they had in the past, the heir is expected to take over the management of the family business, oversee maintenance of the home, and preside over any necessary plans, decisions, or negotiations relating to the core family. When there is no son in a family, the eldest daughter is obligated to assume this position, including marrying a man who will take her family name.

There are several occasions during the year when it is customary for the family to get together. These times include **O-shōgatsu** (New Year's), **O-bon** (a Buddhist celebration in mid-August, honoring the spirits of the dead), and a day selected by the family for **hakamairi** (visiting the gravesite of deceased ancestors), which is often followed by a meal together at home or a nearby inn. (*See also* "Holidays and Festivals.")

30. THE FLAG AND THE NATIONAL ANTHEM

The Japanese flag, called **Nisshōki** or **Hinomaru**, is a solid red circle on a white background. Even on public buildings, the flag is flown only on national holidays. On other days, public buildings fly their own local (municipal or regional) flags, although a few public buildings may choose to fly both their own and the **Hinomaru**. Major companies fly company flags, called **shaki**. Hotels and other companies that deal internationally may fly flags from various countries.

It is not common to see the Japanese flag used as a decorative motif for clothing or artwork, as it would be considered disrespectful.

The national anthem is **Kimi ga yo**, meaning "Thy Reign," and it is sung only on solemn and official occasions. Applause never follows the anthem, and there is no custom of placing the hand over the heart, although it is customary to stand when the anthem is played. As with the flag, respect for the national anthem precludes the composition of musical variations or frivolous uses.

31. FLOWERS AND PLANTS

Part of the traditional Japanese character is a strong appreciation for both the creations and the forces of nature. Popular hobbies are **bonsai** (growing miniature trees in landscaped environments) and **ikebana** (flower arranging), and competition is taken quite seriously. Local shrines, community centers, and merchants often sponsor exhibitions for citizens to display their work.

Although most homes have only limited space for yards or gardens, care is taken to make the most of the space available, and most families with any space at all plant trees, bushes, or smaller shrubs, as well as vegetables and herbs. Although Japanese gardens do not include the abundance of colorful blossoms that characterize the Western garden concept, cut flowers are valued and are often used to celebrate special occasions, as **o-miyage** (presents or souvenirs) when visiting friends, and on Buddhist home altars next to photos of deceased family members. **Hanaya** (flower shops) are a frequent sight in local shopping areas and on busy city streets.

The Japanese strongly associate certain flowers with certain months, and most calendars with floral illustrations adhere closely to these traditional associations. Some flowers and plants that have special significance in Japan include the following:

Sakura (cherry tree)   Internationally known, together with the chrysanthemum, as the Japanese national flower, this decorative cherry is an early and picturesque bloomer. (*See* "Cherry Blossoms and Flower Viewing.")

Kiku (chrysanthemum)   The chrysanthemum is a symbol of the Imperial Family. In **samurai** (warrior class) times, flowers and plants were common selections for **mon** (family crests), which were incorporated into military banners and accoutrements; clothing, furniture, and architectural design; as well as identification seals and other official uses.

Shōbu (iris)   A favorite of many, this beauty figures in much Japanese art, both traditional and modern. Its leaves are artistic symbols for the samurai sword, and its colors, which range from white to deep purple, are considered manly. Its season lasts about three weeks in late May and early June, attracting large crowds of viewers to such places as **Meiji Jingū** (the shrine of the Emperor Meiji), and **Shinjuku Gyoen**   (Shinjuku Imperial Garden) in Tokyo, as well as a number of **shōbu-en** (iris gardens) throughout Japan.

Take (bamboo)   This plant has both decorative and practical uses in Japan and is common in both home and traditional public gardens. Tender bamboo shoots are an edible delicacy, and bamboo leaves are used as food wrappers. The wood of the bamboo is used for light construction and carpentry, and miscellaneous uses include chopsticks, umbrella ribs, window blinds, flower vases, bird- and cricket-cages, and a myriad other items.

Hinoki (Japanese cypress)   Probably the most extensively used of Japan's broad variety of evergreen and broadleaf trees, the cypress's light weight and pleasant aroma make it popular for many personal and household articles, including **geta** (wooden sandals) and **o-furo** (bathtubs). Although it is very expensive, it is sometimes used for interior paneling and other light construction in the home.

32. FOOD AND EATING

The three customary meals in Japan are **asagohan** or **chōshoku** (breakfast), **hirugohan, chūshoku** or **ranchi** (lunch) and **bangohan** or **yūshoku** (the evening meal). Meals usually include rice, although American and European breakfast foods are quite popular, and even the Emperor Showa confessed that he enjoyed bacon and eggs. Dessert is not part of the traditional Japanese meal, but fruit and sometimes sherbet are served as dessert today.

Western visitors may find some items that delight the Japanese palate a bit strange. Many find, however, that a taste for even the most foreign-appearing foodstuffs can be acquired fairly quickly. **Sushi**, bite-sized morsels of cooked rice with a topping of **sashimi** (raw fish) or other seafood, has become quite popular internationally, along with some other dishes, such as **tenpura** (deep-fried shrimp and vegetables) and **sukiyaki** (a savory meat-and-vegetable dish).

O-hashi (chopsticks)   Restaurants that specialize in Western foods will always have Western utensils available as well. Those that offer only chopsticks can usually come up with a spoon for diners who have not yet mastered the art of eating Japanese-style.

Chopsticks come in various styles. The Japanese kind are tapered to a rounded point at the working end, and are often polished and lacquered. Chinese chopsticks are usually squared off at the tip and a little longer than the Japanese variety. There are also **waribashi**, throwaway chopsticks made of light wood, that have to be split apart before use. (Hence the name, which means "divided chopsticks.")

The ability to use chopsticks for eating and cooking requires time and practice to build the appropriate muscles and motor skills in the fingers, hand, and wrist before it becomes second nature. One chopstick is placed in the crook of the thumb and stabilized by the tip of the thumb and one other finger, usually the middle finger or the ring finger. The other chopstick is held more or less as you would hold a pencil. The bottom chopstick is held stable, while the upper chopstick is moved up and down in a pinching maneuver to grasp the desired item. (*See also* "Table Etiquette.")

33. FOOTWEAR

In the **genkan** (entryway) of a Japanese home, both family members and guests are expected to remove their street shoes and put on slippers provided by the family and kept at the door, usually on a shelf or in a cabinet for the purpose. The street shoes are left on the floor of the entry, with the toes facing out to facilitate changing back into them before leaving the house. Slippers are worn on wooden, tiled, or carpeted areas of the house but are removed before entering a **tatami** (rice straw "mat" flooring) room. Bathrooms have their own special slippers (often made of a water-resistant material) that are never worn outside that room. Slippers outside the bathroom door are an indication that the room is occupied.

Walking in slippers calls for a sliding style, since the slippers are usually large enough to be worn by teens to adults of all sizes. Foreigners sometimes find the slippers too short, in which case stocking feet are acceptable in most rooms. Under no circumstances should a person go beyond the **genkan** in street shoes—even in tennis shoes.

During warm summer months, many people go barefoot in their own homes and sockless for casual outdoor wear. Sport shoes are also very popular among young people, but because lacing and unlacing can be cumbersome when going in and out of the house, school, shops, and other places, the shoe is often worn as if it were a slipper, with the heel folded down under the foot.

Other commonly worn Japanese footwear include **zōri** and **geta** (thong-type sandals made of straw or wood) and **tsukkake** (sandals without back-straps).

Visitors at temples, monasteries, and other historical sites are usually asked to remove their street shoes before entering any of the buildings. When the exit is separate from the entrance to such a place, the visitors may be given a bag to carry their shoes in while they walk on the highly polished floors in their stocking feet. Otherwise, there may be a shelf where the shoes can be left at the entryway.

In small clinics, schools, and official buildings in rural areas, visitors are often asked to remove their shoes and use slippers provided for them.

34. FOREIGNERS

Words used to refer to people from other countries include **gaikokujin, gaijin**, and **gaikoku no hito**, and none of these words has any inherent disparaging connotation. Because of the homogeneous character of the Japanese people, foreigners—including some Asians, if they have non-Japanese features—stand out and are often the object of attention. Although it is understandable that this would make many people feel uncomfortable, it should not be taken as a sign of animosity. On the contrary, most Japanese are curious in a very positive way about foreigners and foreign cultures and will go out of their way to be of assistance to strangers in their midst.

35. GENDER ROLES

Although Japan has been a male-dominated society for centuries, the concept of ''equal rights'' for women is not one that is considered by the Japanese to be incongruous with their culture, and women have had great influence in all aspects of society throughout Japanese history.

Nearly half of Japan's work force is female, though women still are not commonly seen in corporate executive positions. Many housewives work in light industry, usually as a part-time supplement to the family income. Single women frequently take jobs as ōeru ("O.L.," for "office lady"), often as a stopgap until they marry. There are also many women, particularly singles, who work toward career goals in politics, business, medicine, education, the media, and the arts, as well as service-related fields, although career is often set aside for marriage and family considerations.

Historically, women have often been quietly considered the "power behind the throne," performing a necessary function as helpers for their husbands, nurturers and teachers of their children, home managers, and keepers of the family exchequer. Men have fulfilled the role of provider and protector, as well as being leaders and governors, both within the family and in society at large. The distinction between men and women has been and still is, for the most part, appreciated and accepted by both sexes.

36. GEOGRAPHY

Japan consists of four main islands, the **Ryūkyū** archipelago that makes up Okinawa, and more than 3,000 islands and islets. The largest of the main islands is **Honshū**, followed by the northern island of **Hokkaidō**, **Kyūshū** on the west end, and **Shikoku** across the Inland Sea from the international port of Kobe.

Only about 25 percent of Japan's land is suitable for settlement and cultivation, the rest being mountainous, including about 50 active volcanoes; and forests cover about 70 percent of the total land area. A dormant volcano, Mount Fuji, is Japan's highest mountain, rising to over twelve thousand feet. The islands are actually the peaks of submerged mountain ranges and are part of a large zone of earthquakes and volcanic activity. (*See* "Earthquakes.")

The largest lowland area is the **Kantō** Plain, with Tokyo at its southern edge. Osaka and Kyoto are located on the lowlands of **Kan-**

sai, and Nagoya is on the **Nobi** Plain. Many smaller coastal plains surround the Inland Sea.

Japan's range of climates is comparable to that of the east coast of North America, and average annual precipitation is about 50 inches, much of which falls during the **tsuyu** (rainy season) from mid-June to mid-July. Typhoons are likely to occur from mid-August through early October.

37. GIFTS

Gift exchange is done in a relatively ritualistic, formal, and sometimes elaborate manner. Ceremonious gift-exchange takes place when receiving delegations and others on official visits. Gifts are given when visiting friends at home, when returning from a trip, when seeing someone off on a trip, and at certain special times of the year. (See below.)

Gifts are both presented and received with both hands, accompanied by a bow of appropriate depth. The gift itself is referred to by the giver as merely "a small token," "small expression," or "a thought" regardless of its monetary value. Some phrases to use when offering a gift include the following:

Tsumaranai mono desu ga. . . It's really nothing.

Kimochi dake desu ga. . . It's just a token (of my feelings).

Konna mono mezurashiku arimasen ga. . . This is really nothing special.

Chiisai mono de hazukashii desu ga. . . I'm embarrassed that this is such a small gift.

When a gift is received, the custom is NOT to open the package unless the giver or others strongly urge that it be opened. Then the recipient may say, "I'll do it American-style," and proceed to unwrap the gift, but only after admiring the packaging. The ribbon and paper are then painstakingly removed, and the gift is finally unveiled with a certain degree of fanfare. While the giver makes such self-deprecating remarks as those given above, the recipient praises the gift and the giver with expressions of gratitude.

Gifts of money are presented in special envelopes that can be purchased at book stores, stationery stores, and train kiosks, as well as in department stores. Congratulatory gift envelopes (**keiji-yō no noshibukuro**) are wrapped and tied with red-and-white, red-and-gold, or gold-and-silver cords, while condolence gift envelopes (**chōji-yō no noshibukuro**) must be black-and-white or silver-and-white.

O-senbetsu and O-miyage   When someone embarks on a trip, particularly overseas, friends will see the person off with a money envelope or items for use while traveling. This kind of gift is called o-senbetsu. When the traveler returns, he will bring back o-miyage (souvenir gifts) for friends, often local specialties from the places he has visited. **O-miyage** are also presented when visiting friends outside Japan, and small gifts are brought back from sightseeing, hiking, or business trips within Japan. For trips within the country, usually **o-senbetsu** are not given unless the trip is to be extensive.

Chūgen and Seibo   Shortly before **O-bon** in the summer and again at year's end, it is traditional for individuals to give gifts to teachers or superiors at work, and companies to give tokens of appreciation to clients and major customers. The summer gift is called o-chūgen, and the winter gift, **o-seibo**. These gifts are sold in a special section of department stores during the appropriate seasons. The store takes care of packaging and delivery of boxed items, including calligraphic renderings of the sender's name on the traditional wrapping.

Temiyage   When visiting someone's home, it is common for the Japanese to take a small gift of fruit, flowers, candy, and so on. Such gifts can be purchased at or near the transit station of the visitor's destination.

O-tsukaimono   These are gifts for special occasions, such as weddings, graduation, housewarming parties, and so forth. Again, department stores will gift-wrap the item for you if you inform the clerk that it is **o-tsukaimono**.

Otoshidama   Children eagerly look forward to their New Year's **otoshidama** (money envelopes) from grandparents, parents, and other adult relatives or close family friends. These are distributed when families visit one another during the first three days of the year.

Others   The American Valentine's Day (**Barentain Dē**) notion recently introduced in Japan has taken its own turn, finding popularity especially among female office workers, who give gifts of chocolate to the men in the office. Cards are not commonly exchanged, except sometimes between young lovers. On March 14, called "White Day" (**Howaito Dē**), male workers reciprocate with white chocolate or other white treats, white symbolizing purity of feeling.

38. GOVERNMENT

Although the government of Japan is called a "constitutional monarchy" and the Imperial Family has maintained a position of influence and even reverence in Japan for longer than any other monarchy in the world, seldom has the Emperor had any particular say in the actual governing of the country.

The end of World War II brought occupation by the Allied Forces under General Douglas MacArthur and the creation and enforcement of a new constitution, which serves the nation to the present time. The constitution provided a bill of rights comparable to that of the United States Constitution and refashioned the Diet into a popularly elected democratic parliament, a bicameral body composed of a House of Representatives and a House of Councillors. The executive body consists of a cabinet headed by a prime minister, who also heads the majority political party. A supreme court of 15 justices comprises the judicial body. The Emperor publicly denied any divine lineage and took a more symbolic role, precluding any real influence in government affairs.

Japan has 47 "prefectures"—comparable to states—plus the

Tokyo capital district. Each prefecture has its own elected **chiji** (governor) and assembly, and all citizens over the age of 20 are eligible to vote.

39. HELLOS AND GOODBYES

Basic greetings include the following standard phrases:
Ohayō gozaimasu. Good morning.
Konnichi wa. Hello (in the daytime).
Konban wa. Good evening.

When you are meeting someone you haven't seen in some time, appropriate phrases are:
Shibaraku desu. It's been a long time.
Gobusata shite imasu I'm sorry for not keeping in touch.

Weather comments normally follow an initial greeting:
Ii o-tenki desu, ne. It's nice weather, isn't it?
Yoku furimasu, ne. It rains/snows a lot, doesn't it?
Henna o-tenki desu, ne. It's terrible, strange weather, isn't it?

Farewells include the following:
Sayōnara. Goodbye.
Jā mata. See you later.
Shitsurei itashimasu. / Shitsurei shimasu. I'm leaving.

The phrase **Itte kimasu** or **Itte mairimasu** (I'll be back) is used when a family member leaves the house for work, school, shopping, and so forth. Those remaining respond with **Itte irasshai** (Come back). **Tadaima** (I'm back) is the phrase used when the person returns home—the others responding **Okaerinasai** (Welcome back). These phrases can also be used in any group setting when a member of the group is going away temporarily.

A standard phrase used by a visitor at the door is **Gomen kudasai**, which is roughly equivalent to ''Is anybody here?''

40. HOLIDAYS AND FESTIVALS

Government offices and many businesses are closed on public holidays, although restaurants and most stores, as well as major public museums, remain open. Nearly all businesses, except necessary or emergency services, close during the New Year's celebration, January 1 to 3. If a national holiday falls on a Sunday, the Monday that follows it becomes a holiday.

There are many local festivals throughout the year, usually centered around neighborhood Shinto shrines and Buddhist temples. (*See* "Shrines and Temples.") These festivals (**o-matsuri**) are celebrations of the changing seasons, planting, and harvesting, with prayers for family health, good fortune and prosperity, and so on. They often include folk dancing (**odori**), carnival-like games and food booths, archery and other martial arts demonstrations, or colorful **mikoshi** (portable shrine) processions, with multitudes of costumed participants chanting and carrying the shrine through the streets. Such local festivities are free to watch, although a fee may be charged for special exhibits or demonstrations, as well as for food and drink.

National Holidays

O-shōgatsu (New Year's)   The most important holiday in Japan, the first three days of January are spent with family members, eating, playing, chatting, and enjoying the time together. Homes at this time are decorated with pieces of straw rope and pine branches, and many families don their best **kimono** to make their first visit of the year (**hatsumōde**) to local shrines and temples to participate in the festivities there and offer prayers for the upcoming year. Some families will burn incense at the **butsudan** (home altar) and offer the first prayer of the year for deceased relatives, so that their spirits will rest in peace and will protect the living. Shinto believers will offer the first cup of fresh water of the year and ask for a blessing from the spirits. Catholics will attend mass to fulfill their holy day obligation. Still others believe that seeing the first sunrise from atop Mount Fuji will bring the best fortune.

On New Year's morning the family gathers around the table to share good wishes and take a ceremonious sip of **o-toso** (sweet wine served only on this day). Also shared during the day are **ozōni**, a soup of vegetables and meat or seafood poured over a cake of pounded sweet rice (**mochi**), and **o-sechi ryōri**, a meal of over 20 dishes prepared according to traditional symbolism.

Children are given good-luck gifts (**otoshidama**) of money at New Year's. In rural areas youngsters are able to enjoy traditional New Year's games, such as **hane-tsuki** (similar to badminton), **tako-age** (kite-flying), **karuta** (a card game using Japanese phrases), and **koma-mawashi** (top-spinning). In the cities, however, although the toys themselves are sold in downtown stores and displayed prominently in the home, games that require much space are not played.

Seijin no Hi (Adults' Day)   People who have reached 20 years of age over the previous year are honored and officially accepted as adults on January 15, attending a formal ceremony held at the local government office, where each young adult officially accepts responsibility as a citizen. It is also looked on as a photo opportunity, and copies of pictures taken at this occasion are often sent to relatives and friends. Gifts of money are presented in some families, and for daughters a set of traditional kimono may be made.

Kenkoku Kinenbi (National Foundation Day)   February 11 is the day when, according to tradition, **Jinmu Tennō** became the first emperor in 660 B.C. (*See* "The Imperial Family.")

Shunbun no Hi (Vernal Equinox)   On this day (March 20 or 21), the coming of spring is celebrated. Many families visit the family burial plot at this time and join extended family members for dinner together afterwards.

Midori no Hi (Arbor Day)   Literally "Day of Green," April 29 is also the birthday of the late Emperor Shōwa, known to most of the world as Hirohito. This day begins a period called **Gōruden Uiiku** (Golden Week), which includes three national holidays. Highways, transit systems, and hotels are very crowded at this time, as people go on vacation, visit relatives and friends, and are generally on the move.

Kenpō Kinenbi (Constitution Day)   May 3 marks the anniversary of the post-World War II Constitution written while Japan was under Allied Occupation. (*See* "Government.")

Kodomo no Hi (Children's Day)   May 5 marks a relatively new day of celebration for all children, combining the traditional Girls' Day (March 3: *See* Hina Matsuri/Doll Festival) and Boys' Festival into one national holiday. Originating in the 17th century, **Tango no Sekku** (Boys' Festival) was celebrated on May 5. Families with boys fly colorful streamers and banners in the image of carp, symbolizing perseverance and strength as desirable attributes for young boys growing into manhood. In the home, miniature figures of legendary warriors from Japan's feudal period are displayed on tiered stands along with their armor, banners, and swords.

Keirō no Hi   (Respect-for-the-Elderly Day) September 15 is set aside as a reminder of the contributions of Japan's senior citizens.

Shūbun no Hi (Autumnal Equinox)   On this day, which falls on September 23 or 24, visits (**hakamairi**) are made to gravesites of relatives and good friends. Many people make their annual family visit to the gravesite either on this day or on the day of Vernal Equinox.

Taiiku no Hi (Sports Day)   October 10 is kept as a reminder that sports and exercise are a means of maintaining physical and mental health. This holiday is marked by contests and games of both competitive and noncompetitive nature.

Bunka no Hi (Culture Day)   On November 3 the nation honors those who have made special contributions toward peace and freedom or in academic or cultural pursuits. It was originally celebrated as the birthday of Emperor Meiji, under whose reign (1868 to 1912) Japan's first constitution was established.

Kinrō Kansha no Hi (Labor Appreciation Day) Japan honors its workers on November 23. In some parts of the country, this day is celebrated with harvest festivals.

Tennō Tanjō no Hi (Emperor's Birthday) December 23 marks the anniversary of the birth of the current Emperor Akihito. (*See* "The Imperial Family.")

Other Holidays

There are local holidays and festivals in various parts of Japan throughout the year. However, a few of these have national significance and are celebrated widely, even though they are not official national holidays.

Setsubun (Bean-throwing ritual)   On the last day of winter, February 3 or 4, people flock to major local temples and shrines to participate in this rite to "drive away devils" and to herald the coming of spring. Also, many households continue the tradition of opening windows and throwing out a handful of roasted soybeans while chanting **Oni wa soto** (Out, evil spirits!), then tossing beans inside the house with the cry **Fuku wa uchi** (Inside, good fortune!). Eating a number of beans equivalent to one's own age plus one is believed to bring good fortune.

Hina Matsuri (Doll Festival)   Originally called **Momo no Sekku** (Festival of Peach Blossoms), on this day, March 3, young girls (and their mothers) enjoy **hina ningyō**, dolls dressed up in ancient costumes, representing the Emperor, the Empress, and their household. The dolls are set up on tiered display shelves, along with miniature pieces of furniture. **Hina ningyō** are usually a gift from the maternal grandmother when a baby girl is born, and some sets are handed down over many generations. Tradition dictates that the dolls must be carefully put away within three days after the festival or the young girl will miss her chance for marriage.

Although not a national holiday, it is celebrated widely with special foods prepared at home, plus sweets and crackers that are sold in the stores only at this time.

Hana Matsuri (Buddha's Birthday)   April 8 is observed through-out Japan in Buddhist temples and generally coincides with the blos-soming of flowers in the spring. At this time a statue of the Child Buddha is decorated with garlands of flowers, placed in a special wide, shallow basin, and **amacha** (sweet tea) is poured over the statue with a ladle.

Mei Dei (Worker's Day)   Borrowed from the English "May Day," this day, May 1, during Golden Week is celebrated by unions and Socialists and Communist political partisans with marches, picnics, and political speeches.

Tanabata (Festival of Stars) According to an ancient Chinese legend, the Weaver Star (Vega) and the Shepherd Star (Altair) are lovers who are allowed to meet once a year on July 7. If the sky is overcast, and the stars cannot be seen, the meeting does not take place until the following year. It is customary to offer seasonal fruits and vegeta-bles to the stars on this evening and to decorate bamboo branches with poems or proverbs written on strips of colorful paper by the school-age children in the home. The bamboo branch is then placed by the front entrance to the house.

In recent years the **Tanabata** festival has been popularized by merchants, and many shopping areas compete with elaborate decorations.

O-bon (All Souls' Festival)   Held in mid-August (mid-July in some rural areas), this festival celebrates the spirits of the dead, who are believed to return to their homes at this time. The living also return to their hometowns, and traditional dances and other activities are held. Transportation facilities are very crowded during this period.

Shichi-go-san (Children's Shrine-Visiting Day)   The name **Shichi-go-san** means "7-5-3" and refers to 7-year-old girls, 5-year-old boys, and 3-year olds of both genders, who are dressed in their best clothing and taken to Shinto shrines on November 15 by their parents to offer thanks for good health and to receive blessings for the future.

Year's End   Not specifically a holiday, the last two weeks of December are still very festive as the Japanese wind up the old year and prepare for the new. Year-end cleaning is done in homes, and merchants enjoy a brisk sale season, as many companies give their employees bonuses—often equal to two or three times their monthly salary—at this time of year. Companies also sponsor **bōnenkai** (year-end parties), where plenty of food and drink is provided and employees and their bosses are encouraged to let their hair down and enjoy a fun and informal evening together.

Ōmisoka (New Year's Eve)   Many families gather at shrines or at homes before midnight to usher in the new year on December 31. The mood is quiet and reflective, and a number of traditions are carried out during the day, including last-minute straightening-up and opening the windows momentarily to rid the house of "last-year's dust." Another tradition is the eating of **toshikoshi soba** (buckwheat noodles, the length symbolizing longevity), and as midnight approaches, young children beg parents for permission to stay up to hear the **joya no kane**, 108 resonant gongs from a nearby temple bell (or from a well-known temple via TV). While the bell tolls, each person reflects on the events of the passing year and his or her hopes for the one to come, and as the last gong resonates, New Year's greetings are exchanged: **Shinnen omedetō gozaimasu** or **Akemashite omedetō gozaimasu** or simply "Happy New Year" in English. A more recent tradition is the performance of Beethoven's Ninth Symphony by a major Japanese orchestra on this evening.

41. HONORIFIC SPEECH (*KEIGO*)

Despite the official equality that currently exists in Japanese society, there is still a strong tradition of respectful expression that goes beyond the Western concept of courtesy. On a basic level, anything that belongs to the speaker is abased, while anything that pertains to the person to whom one is speaking is exalted. Typical of this is the use of prefixes **o-** and **go-** and choosing appropriate verb endings according to the degree of politeness required.

Most Japanese language courses emphasize the ''normal-polite'' level of speech, and it is advisable for foreigners to stick to this level until skilled enough in both language and culture to begin incorporating some of the more honorific expressions. This level of speech includes a degree of courtesy that is acceptable for foreigners to use in any situation, since the Japanese people are very aware of the fact that most foreigners struggle to speak Japanese at all, much less understand the complicated rules of **keigo**.

42. HOTELS AND INNS

Although there are many Western-style hotels in Japan, there are also numerous inns that maintain the traditional style of Japanese hospitality and ambience. Called **ryokan**, each has its own specialty: scenic view, hot springs, gourmet cuisine, and so forth. Fees are on the expensive side and are charged according to the number of nights per person, with breakfast, dinner, amenities, and taxes included. Families and groups may be given a lower per-person rate if they are staying together.

Guests' rooms are an extension of the traditional Japanese living style, with **tatami** (rice-straw mat) flooring and **futon** (a thin mattress and comforter, usually laid on the floor) bedding. Sliding doors are unlockable, but many establishments provide a small safe in each room for securing personal items. Otherwise, guests may store valuables in a vault located on the premises.

Both service and food are generally superb and the atmosphere serene. Maids are available to help with such things as laying out bedding, taking care of light laundry needs, and bringing meals, which are delivered to the guest's room. The maid may also stay to serve the meal and even to explain items of local history and lore. Meals are planned by the chef, and there are usually few or no alternative choices and no menu.

Toilet and bathing facilities—Japanese style—are in common areas, a practice not always comfortable to foreign visitors. Both bath and meals are available only during specified hours. A **yukata** (cotton kimono to relax in while at the inn) and, in cold weather, a **tanzen** (quilted kimono worn over the **yukata**) may be provided, along with towels and other common amenities. Towels provided by **ryokan** are usually **tenugui**, made of light terry-cloth and measuring approximately 13 inches by 35 inches, with the name and logo of the inn printed on them. **Tenugui** are used as both washcloth and drying towel. (A wet **tenugui** must be wrung out several times by the bather to be effective in the drying process.) It is acceptable for **tenugui** to be taken home as a souvenir; however, the **yukata** and **tanzen** should not be taken without paying for them.

Hotels   Western-style hotels (**hoteru**) are plentiful in Japan, and services are comparable to those found in the West. There are also motels (**mōteru**), but these are, for the most part, among those hostels classified as **rabu-hoteru** (love hotels) with rooms rented by the hour and often with elaborate, sexually oriented furnishings, services, and amenities.

Minshuku   There are many registered **minshuku** throughout Japan, comparable to the Western "bed & breakfast" concept, for those who wish to try "real" country living. Accommodations are Spartan by Western standards, but the experience can be rewarding.

43. HOUSING AND FURNISHINGS

Most Japanese live in apartments (**apāto**) or condominiums (**man-shon**), rather than independent houses (**ie**). This is largely due to the exorbitant costs of land and construction. Large companies may provide basic, low-cost **shataku** housing, usually consisting of multiple buildings with perhaps hundreds of apartments in each. Young couples often take advantage of this housing for the first few years of marriage, until they can afford something better. For single employees, company dormitories (**ryō**) may be provided.

Homes always include a **genkan** (entryway), where visitors and family alike pause to change shoes and announce their arrival. Often there will be a **noren** (a short curtain) hanging from the top of the doorway that leads into the main body of the home.

Standard flooring for rooms beyond the **genkan** is **tatami**, mats of rice straw where neither shoes nor slippers are allowed. Hallways are usually floored in wood, which is kept well polished; kitchens have either wood or linoleum flooring; and bathrooms are ceramic-tiled and have a drain to allow for the water that is splashed and poured during the bathing process.

Some older homes and low-rent apartments do not include bathing areas, and a few still utilize indoor open-pit toilets, which must be emptied periodically into special tank trucks and taken to disposal areas. Most family homes, however, have more modern amenities.

Walls are usually plastered, and since central heating is not the norm for private homes, rooms are individually heated and cooled with space heaters and fans or other small air conditioning units. Outside walls must, therefore, be porous enough to allow the structure to "breathe," and even in cold weather, windows are often left open a few inches.

In older homes, entrance may be through a sliding door; apartments and newer homes have Western-style wood or steel doors and doorways, including deadbolts and peepholes. Room and closet doors may be Western-style or, especially in older construction, sliding, paper-paneled doors (**karakami**).

Yards and gardens, even around independent houses, are rarely larger than a few square meters, and grass lawns are not common. Any available space is carefully, if not meticulously, landscaped. Urban and suburban houses are surrounded by walls or hedges, and there is often an intercom system to allow residents to screen visitors before allowing them entrance. Rural homes are frequently more open, and plants often include vegetables, as well as ornamentals.

In rural, agricultural areas, there can still be seen the occasional thatched-roof structure—picturesque, but requiring considerable maintenance, as thatch is not as durable as the ceramic tile that tops most residences.

Japanese home furnishings have adapted more and more to Western styles since the Meiji Era, but many people still find traditional items more to their liking. Among the popular standards are the following:

Futon—bedding that consists of a thin mattress that is laid on the soft **tatami** flooring and topped with a fluffy "comforter"-type covering. (Stepping on **futon** is considered poor manners.)

Tansu—a distinctly Japanese-style chest of drawers, an ideal way to store **kimono**.

Kotatsu—a short-legged table with an electric heater attached to the underside, with a sort of blanket that hangs to the floor from underneath the table top. (A more ancient version was built over a pit where hot coals were heaped. Diners sat around the table and dangled their feet over the coals or rested them on a built-in shelf near the top of the pit.)

Zabuton—cushions that take the place of chairs in any room that has **tatami** flooring. (Like **futon**, these also should not be stepped on.) A more comfortable innovation is the legless chair (**zaisu**), which provides back support for the user.

Butsudan—the family altar for paying respect to one's ancestors, reflecting the influence of Buddhism in the daily life of most Japanese.

Kamidana—Shinto altar that hangs high on the wall, reachable by means of a footstool.

Tokonoma—a decorative alcove with a low ledge, usually adorned with a hanging scroll (**kakemono**), classical flower arrangement (**ikebana**), or other *objets d'art*. The **tokonoma** is usually the only raised area found in the traditional room, and although it is inviting, it must *never* be used for sitting.

44. HUMOR

The Japanese sense of humor is so strongly based in the traditional culture that it is not only difficult to translate, but difficult for members of other cultures to understand, even with the best of interpretations. Still, there is a great appreciation for humor evident throughout Japanese history, from the **Amaterasu Ōmikami** legend (*See* "The Imperial Family.") through the court jesters of the Middle Ages, to the traditional **Kabuki** and **Nō** theatrical forms (*See* "Theater.")

Although **rakugo** (comic story-telling) and **manzai** (comic stage dialogue, a la vaudeville) have seen their best years, they still maintain a following, and there are annual special television broadcasts during the New Year holiday season, as well as fan clubs (**rakugo aikōsha no kai**) at some universities. **Rakugo** involves a single comedian, dressed in traditional kimono, sitting on the floor in center stage, describing and repeating humorous conversations among two or more absent characters. In classic **rakugo**, scripts are handed down from artist to trainee, and comic pieces by specific **meijin** (master performers) continue to be enjoyed for generations. Modern **rakugo** treats current events, but dialogue is delivered in the classic **rakugo** style. Two kinds of **rakugo** developed over the years—**Kantō** style, spoken in the Tokyo working-class dialect, and **Kansai** style, spoken in Osaka dialect.

Manzai, which developed in the **Kansai** area, has no rigid or inherited script, but only predetermined topics and key points that are treated by two or three performers together. There is no tradition of artist-to-trainee succession with **manzai**.

Individually, the Japanese enjoy a good joke or funny story and are especially fond of **kotoba no share** (puns and other word-plays), which are used liberally in advertising and product names. Satire is also well appreciated, and favorite subjects are political issues and other current events. Unlike Westerners, however, speakers never begin serious speeches, lectures, or business discussions with "ice-breaker" jokes or anecdotes, although humor is appropriately used during the course of a presentation to develop rapport with the audience.

45. THE IMPERIAL FAMILY

The first written chronicles of Japanese history give 660 B.C. as the date when **Jinmu Tennō** became the first emperor of Japan. The legend declares that two deities, **Izanagi-no-Mikoto** and **Izanami-no-Mikoto**, descended from heaven to create the islands of Japan. The sun goddess **Amaterasu Ōmikami** eventually sent her grandson **Ninigi-no-Mikoto** to rule over Japan, sending with him sacred regalia as symbols of his authority. These included a mirror, symbol of the sun; a jewel, representing the moon; and a sword, representing lightning. Three generations later, **Jinmu Tennō**, the great grandson of Ninigi-no-Mikoto, inherited these items when he became the first to ascend the throne.

Until the end of World War II, the Imperial Family was believed to be directly descended from this divine source. Despite the disavowal of divine origin by Emperor Hirohito (now **Shōwa Tennō**) soon after the conclusion of World War II, the emperorship has retained a degree of popular respect and reverence possibly unequaled in the world.

The current Emperor Akihito, whose posthumous name will be **Heisei Tennō**, carries on the long imperial tradition with the blessing of the vast majority of the people, although a few in recent years have debated the appropriateness of this type of monarchy in the modern age. Emperor Akihito, referred to by the Japanese as simply **Tennō Heika** (His Majesty the Emperor), who inherited the throne in 1989, was the first in the imperial line to marry a commoner, now the Empress Michiko, whom he met on the tennis court as a university student. They have two sons—Crown Prince Naruhito Hironomiya and Prince Fumihito Ayanomiya—and one daughter, Princess Saya-ko Norinomiya, the youngest of the three.

46. INDIVIDUALS AND COUPLES

When a baby is born to a couple, the family unit expands to include the baby. An example of the extended-couple concept is a young couple celebrating their wedding anniversary by dining out at a restaurant with their children along for the occasion. The idea of having a baby-sitter has not taken root in Japan, and grandparents or a relative are more likely to be called on to watch the children on those infrequent occasions when parents must attend events alone.

Dining out and going for drinks are very much a part of the business world, but spouses are rarely present on those occasions unless it is a very special event. A man may bring home a few colleagues for snacks and drinks; however, his wife will not ordinarily join in the fellowship, but will maintain a separate role as hostess. Women choose to go out together, usually during daytime hours when children are in school or in conjunction with PTA or other group activities.

47. INTRODUCTIONS AND NETWORKING

Networking is an important business practice in any culture, but it is especially so in Japan. Business networking in Japan is primarily a closed system, with contacts maintained in a formal manner and within a tightly knit group. The process of networking is called **nema-washi** (literally, "digging around the roots"). When seeking employment in Japan, knowing the right people and having good letters of introduction (**shōkaijō**) are paramount, and preliminary research is essential to developing a beneficial network.

Name-dropping or bragging about who wrote your letter of recommendation is considered inappropriate. A less formal way of creating a new contact is for a mutual friend to write a short note on his own business card, in place of a letter of introduction.

When entering the Japanese business world as a foreigner, it is important to learn to recognize and work within the Japanese system. After initial introductions are made, it is necessary to be both patient and persistent. For example, it can be beneficial to stop by someone's office to say hello or do small favors for colleagues, such as offering to help write English correspondence, answering questions about English language and culture studies, gathering information from the United States for them and so forth.

Some good phrases to remember on such short visits to someone's office include the following:

Chotto soko made kita node, yotte mimashita. I happened to be in the vicinity, so I just thought I would drop by.

A, ima o-isogashii desu ka. Jā, mata ukagaimasu. Oh, you are busy now. I'll drop by again some other time.

Arigatō gozaimashita. Shitsurei shimasu. Thank you. I'll be leaving now.

48. KARAOKE

An activity that gained considerable popularity in the United States during the 1980s and 1990s, **karaoke** (from **kara**, meaning "empty" and **oke** borrowed from the English word "*orch*estra") has its origins in Japanese piano bars, where pianists sometimes accommodated patrons who wanted to sing. Recording companies picked up on the idea and began producing music-only tapes of popular tunes. Small rental rooms, called **karaoke bokkusu** ("karaoke box"), acoustically designed and equipped with **karaoke** components, became popular places for people to imitate their favorite singers and have fun with friends.

The **karaoke** bar became a favorite entertainment activity throughout Japan and quickly caught on in Hawaii as well, though it took several years to gain popularity on the U.S. mainland. **Karaoke** etiquette allows even the tone-deaf a moment in the spotlight; however, encores are considered inappropriate, even for the musically talented, if there are others in line for the microphone.

49. LEISURE (*REJĀ*)

Since World War II, "workaholism" in Japan has become a serious enough problem to require the attention of the government, which in recent years has openly campaigned to encourage the **sarariiman** (salaryman, white-collar worker) to forego late hours, take more time off, and do things with his family. Commercials have run on radio and TV, plus print advertisements in public places, extolling the virtues of a well-rested life, in contrast to a growing stereotype of the Japanese businessman as one who spends more time at work than at home, suffers from stress, and is in danger of succumbing to **karōshi** (untimely death from stress and overwork).

Even when the Japanese indulge in leisure sports, travel, hobbies, and other activities, they often go at it as if it were a professional assignment, investing in top-of-the-line equipment, training, and instruction at the hands of pros, and the latest fashions in name-brand casual wear. Even the occasional mountain hike—a popular exercise for all ages—requires a sturdy and colorful knapsack and coordinated clothing, as well as state-of-the-art photographic equipment for souvenir photos that will later be mounted in albums and shared with friends.

50. LETTERS, GREETING CARDS, AND POSTAL SERVICES

Letters   Although addresses written in the Roman alphabet are usually not a problem for mail delivery personnel, if it is important that an item be delivered accurately and quickly—particularly if the destination is not one of the larger metropolitan areas—it is advisable to have someone rewrite the address in the Japanese script, including the three-digit postal code, which is preceded by the symbol 〒 .

Postcards   Both regular postcards (**hagaki**) and picture postcards (**ehagaki**) are charged at a lower rate than letters, as in the United States. Picture postcards are charged letter rate if any portion of the message is written on the address side of the center line.

Money Envelopes   Since checking accounts are not commonly used by individuals or families, bills are usually paid either by automatic withdrawal from the bank account or by sending cash through the mail in special envelopes called **genkin fūtō** (available at post offices), a practice that is generally considered extremely safe.

Greeting Cards   A traditional social obligation is to send special greeting cards to business associates, teachers, relatives, friends, and others at New Year's and again during mid-summer. **Nengajō** (New Year's Cards) are specially prepared postcards, which are mailed the last week of December and held by the post office to be delivered on New Year's Day. The midsummer postcard greeting is called **shochū mimai** (midsummer inquiry) and is essentially inquiring after the health and well-being of acquaintances. These should be mailed before July 15. If that date is missed, **Zansho mimai** (late-summer inquiry) may be sent before mid-August.

Some people order personalized cards, while most purchase appropriate generic cards at stationery stores.

Addresses   When writing an address vertically in Japanese on an envelope or postcard, the largest unit (city and prefecture) is written first, followed by the street address and apartment number, and finally the name of the individual, followed by the suffix **-sama**. When writing horizontally, either Japanese script or romanization, the same order may be used as with an address in English.

Postal Services   The Japanese postal service is prompt and reliable, and post offices carry out a full range of services. Public mailboxes (**posuto**) are available in all urban areas and easy to spot because of their bright orange color. They often have separate slots for local and out-of-town addresses. Clerks at the post office (**yūbinkyoku**) are knowledgeable and will readily give information on postal rates, regulations, and other aspects of mail service; however, they are not known for either their friendliness or their English speaking ability. Home delivery is daily, and all homes have private boxes (**yūbin-bako**) or mail slots (**yūbin'ire**).

51. LOVE AND AFFECTION

Despite a recent trend among Japanese youth toward more Westernized displays of affection, for most Japanese it is still considered unacceptable for couples to engage in kissing, hugging, or even holding hands in front of other people, whether in a public place or indoors. Waves, bows, and verbal expressions are used in greetings and farewells, but no more physical display than that. Girls, however, may walk arm-in-arm with other girls.

It also is not common for husbands and wives to tell each other "I love you" in so many words. Foreigners should also be very careful about verbalizing affection for a Japanese person. The term **Suki desu**, which literally means "I like you," is used by the Japanese to express romantic attraction stronger than friendship. A safer alternative is to compliment the person, perhaps with a phrase such as **Tanoshii hito desu, ne** (You're a fun person) or **Tanoshikatta** (or **Omoshirokatta**) **desu** (It's been fun/I had a great time), or simply to include the person in off-hours activities.

Appropriate phrases for expressing romantic love include the following:

Daisuki desu. I like/love you very much.

Mata issho ni koko ni kitai desu. I want to come back here with you again. (This is comparable in meaning to "I really do love you, and I want a lasting relationship.")

Itsumo issho ni itai desu. I want to be with you always. (This is tantamount to a marriage proposal.)

Whether expressing romantic love or friendly affection, too much verbalization is neither expected nor appreciated.

❁

52. LUCKY AND UNLUCKY NUMBERS

Even numbers are associated with mathematical concepts and mechanical exactness, while uneven numbers are considered to relate more to the asymmetrical beauties of nature. In respect for this concept, when selecting gifts, odd numbers are preferred over even ones for happy occasions. For example, a visitor may take seven pieces of cake as a gift when visiting a friend's house, even if there will be only six people, including the visitor himself.

Gifts at funerals, however, are in even numbers. Other exceptions include sets of "his-and-her" items, as well as teacups, dinnerware, and glasses that are sold in units of a dozen or a half-dozen.

In any case, the number nine is avoided, since the word **ku** (nine) has a homonym that refers to suffering. The number four is also studiously avoided, since **shi** (four) can also mean "death."

❁

53. MALE/FEMALE SPEECH

As in many other countries, men and women in Japan have speech habits and patterns that are typical to the speaker's gender. It is difficult to teach such patterns in any but the most basic terms without creating confusion for the student, and picking up the language informally often leads to the development of habits that are wrong for the gender of the speaker. Students who are at least aware that there is this difference, however, should be able to find a safe enough middle ground to avoid developing inappropriate speech habits.

In general, male speech tends to be more abbreviated, and it includes more informal or shorter forms than women's speech. The pronoun meaning "I" or "me" is expressed **watakushi** or **watashi** by both men and women in polite or formal situations, but in casual speech men use **boku**, and women use **atashi**. Overuse of **wa, yo, wa yo, no yo, no ne** and the like at the end of a sentence is considered effeminate, as is the frequent use of **deshō?** Intonation is also gender-typical, women's speech being generally more expressive of emotion.

54. MONEY

The Japanese monetary unit is the **yen**, or **en** in Japanese. Money denominations are one-, five-, ten-, fifty-, one hundred-, and five hundred-yen coins, plus 1,000-, 5,000-, and 10,000-yen bills. Since the exchange rate fluctuates from day to day, it is advisable to check with a local bank just prior to going to Japan for the most current value.

International credit cards and traveler's checks are honored at major hotels, some stores, and certain restaurants in larger cities, but it is best to keep an adequate supply of Japanese currency on hand. A cashier's check drawn on a US bank and made out to an individual may be cashed at some large banks, but such a transaction takes considerable time, and fees are exorbitant. Japanese individuals do not have personal checking accounts, but deal in cash for most transactions.

55. MT. FUJI

The highest mountain in Japan is **Fuji-san** (Mt. Fuji, **-san** meaning "mount" or "mountain" in this case). Rising 12,388 feet, it is located in Yamanashi Prefecture, only a few hours' train ride from Tokyo. Weather permitting, a view of this majestic mountain can be seen from the **Shinkansen** (Bullet Train) en route between Tokyo and Kyoto—from windows on the right side of the train on the westward route and on the left side when riding eastward to Tokyo. On the **Tōkaidō** line express, Mt. Fuji will come into view—also from right-side windows—after passing Numazu station, about one and one-half hours out of Tokyo.

Watching the sun rise from atop Mt. Fuji is said to be an experience of a lifetime, and many Japanese and visitors alike climb Mt. Fuji for this purpose.

56. MUSIC AND DANCE

Western pop music is very popular among Japan's youth and has spawned numerous imitators—both bands and individual vocalists—many of whom have developed a strong domestic following, although none have become particularly popular elsewhere in the world. Popular dances also generally copy American and European trends.

Older people prefer less electric styles, including traditional **min'yō** and more recent **enka**. Min'yō are folk tunes, many of which call for lively group dancing at local celebrations, such as the midsummer **O-bon** festival. **Enka** are a blend of warbling folk-music styles and adaptations of Western instrumentation, with a heavy emphasis on saxophones and strings. The characteristic "shmaltzy" lyrics—bemoaning lost love and the sufferings of the common man—have caused many to describe **enka** as the "country-western music of Japan." Popular among the over-30 set, **enka** are frequent choices in **karaoke** pubs.

Western classical musicians—Mozart, Beethoven, Schubert, and others—are widely appreciated by the Japanese, and American jazz also has a strong following.

57. MYTHS, LEGENDS, AND FOLKLORE

The Japanese mythological pantheon is replete with fascinating supernatural creatures that have varying degrees and types of magical powers—to say nothing of strange shapes. **Tengu** (beak-nosed mountain goblins) and **kappa** (a scaly river sprite with a plate-shaped attachment on the top of the head) are mischievous at best and often cruel and treacherous. **Kappa** are mischievous pranksters, although they often take on a certain cuteness in the everyday life of children, as a common decorative theme for lunchboxes, toys, and other personal items.

Obake, usually translated ''ghost,'' refers to any type of preternatural being, nearly always unhappy, angry spirits of individuals who met untimely, gory deaths. The cute and friendly benevolent beings that show up frequently in Western literary culture do not occur in Japanese lore.

Other creatures that frequently occur in Japanese myths are animals such as **tanuki** (raccoon-dogs, badger-like mammals that have facial features similar to the raccoon), **kitsune** (foxes), and **saru** (monkeys), all of which have a reputation for mischief, and **tsuru** (cranes), magical birds that often have benevolent, mystical qualities.

Well-known children's tales include the following favorites:
Momotarō (Peach Boy). Born out of the middle of a large peach, **Momotarō** became **Nippon-ichi** (the best/favorite of Japan) after doing battle with the wicked **oni** (devils) on **Onigashima** Island, defeating the demons with the help of a dog, a monkey, and a pheasant met en route, and retrieving the treasures the **oni** had stolen from villagers in their various wicked forays onto the mainland.

Issunbōshi (Little One-Inch) A ''Tom Thumb''-type character who slays the local ogre and rescues a normal-size maiden, gaining not only the praise and gratitude of the ruler of the land (the girl's father) but normal size for himself—and he gets to marry the maiden.

Urashimataro This is a story about a farmer who saves the life of a turtle and is rewarded with a trip to the bottom of the sea, where he gains the favor of an ocean-bound princess who gives him a magic box with strict instructions not to open it—which, of course, he does and suffers the consequences.

Kintaro A strong, healthy boy with a kind heart protects the local forest creatures and is ultimately challenged by a bear to a **sumo** match. The boy wins and subordinates the bear to his own wishes.

❌

58. NAMES, TITLES, AND FORMS OF ADDRESS

The Japanese family name (surname) precedes the given name, opposite to the Western order. There is only one given name.

Given names are used among family members, relatives, and childhood friends. Otherwise, surnames or titles are used. When the surname is used to address someone, it is followed by the honorific suffix **-san** or, in formal or other special situations, **-sama**, which is a higher honorific. Neither **-san** nor **-sama** nor any other honorific suffix should ever be placed after one's own name. It is recommended that foreigners speaking in English stay with the Western forms of address, "Mr.," "Mrs.," and "Miss"/"Ms.," especially in business situations.

In a self-introduction, usually only the family name is given, especially if a **meishi** (business card) is presented at the same time. (In business and formal situations, given names are never used.) Even junior high and high school students, especially young men, often call each other by their surnames. Children and young women are more likely to go by their given name or a diminutive form. Name tags usually carry the person's family name.

People in positions of authority are called by their titles, such as sensei ("teacher," used also for doctors, attorneys, and some other professionals) or **shachō** (company president). Within a family, of course, parents are addressed as **otōsan** (father) and **okāsan** (mother). Older siblings are called **oniisan** (older brother) and **onēsan** (older sister); however, a younger sibling is more likely to be addressed by the given name or a diminutive, followed by the familiar suffix **-chan** (as in **Ken-chan** for "Ken" or **Etchan** for "Etsuko").

Family relationship words are also often used when addressing a stranger. For example, a customer in a store might call a young female clerk **onēsan**. Similarly, an adult may be referred to as **ojisan** (uncle) or **obasan** (aunt). Also, the words **okusan** (wife or lady of the house) and **otōsan** (father) are sometimes used to address an adult woman or man. However, in some situations the employment of any of these terms may not be in the best taste, and so their use in this way should be avoided by foreigners. The safe option is to use the expression **Sumimasen** (Excuse me) to get the attention of any stranger.

A married woman will call her husband **anata** (you), which is comparable to an English speaker addressing her spouse as "Dear." A man will more likely call his wife by her name.

59. NUMBERS AND COUNTING

Arabic Numerals   Although there are **kanji** characters that represent numbers, Arabic numerals are commonly used in day-to-day written communication. (Commas and decimal points are the same as American usage.) **Kanji** numbers are reserved for official documents, historical writings, and a number of other specialized uses.

Counters   When counting things or people, the Japanese use a system of suffixes called "counters" or "classifiers" following the appropriate number. This is similar to English expressions like *ten pieces* of paper, *four loaves* of bread, *one stick* of butter, but the Japanese system is much more extensive and complicated. The counter **-ko**, for example, is used to count small, roundish items (**ikko, niko, sanko** . . .), vehicles are counted by **-dai**, and buildings are counted by **-ken**. Animals are counted using several different counters: **-tō** for large animals, **-hiki** for small animals, and **-wa** for winged animals.

A "general counter" is used for items for which there is no specific counter, or for which the specific counter is unknown: **hitotsu, futatsu, mittsu, yottsu, itsutsu, muttsu, nanatsu, yattsu, kokonotsu, tō**. This counter stops at 10, however, and the usual numbers (**jū-ichi, jū-ni, jū-san** . . .) are used without a counter for items over 10.

Large Numbers   An English speaker may express numbers of four or more digits as either "thousands" or "hundreds" (1,200 = twelve hundred). This is not the practice of the Japanese, however, and 1,200 is **issen-nihyaku** (one thousand two hundred). The numbers 10,000 and over are not expressed in terms of so-many "thousand," but as so-many **man** (ten thousand). To avoid misunderstandings and confusion, numbers beyond 1,000 might best be written down. A good phrase to remember is **Sumimasen, kaite kudasai.** (Excuse me—please write it for me.)

60. ORIENTAL MEDICINE

Very popular among the Japanese is **tōyō igaku** (Oriental medicine), which was first introduced by the Chinese in about the eighth century. Although it relies in part on herbal curatives, it also includes more familiar treatments, such as acupuncture and massage. Specialty shops are common in both urban and rural areas, and many medical doctors work in conjunction with registered practitioners.

61. PINBALL (PACHINKO)

Still a popular pastime in Japan is a kind of upright pinball game called **pachinko**. The player sits in front of the machine and pours an allotment of **tama** (steel balls, smaller than marbles) into a sloping tray, where they roll into position to be catapulted into the machine when the player flips a lever. A lucky player will find the tray refilled from time to time when the **tama** have run their course through the right combination of bumpers, slots, and passages.

At the end of play, any remaining **tama** may be exchanged for candy, cigarettes, or other small items. There are no cash awards given in the **pachinko pārā** (pachinko parlor), but there are places nearby where the reward items can be exchanged for cash. By law, only adults 18 and older are allowed to play **pachinko**.

62. POLITENESS AND RUDENESS

Visitors to Japan are quick to notice that it is a relatively orderly society. Although it is extremely crowded in all metropolitan areas, public altercations are rare, and differences and disagreements are usually settled amicably. Even in the unavoidable traffic jams on city roadways, horns are used to warn pedestrians or other drivers and not to express disapproval or irritation as they are in many crowded cities of the world.

This orderliness and amicability arises undoubtedly from Japan's centuries-old standards of protocol and leaves many visitors with the distinct impression that ''all Japanese are polite.'' Others, however, may be shocked at certain standards of conduct among the Japanese that may not be acceptable in the West. For example, rush hour at the train station seems to bring out the worst in people as they deliberately push and shove one another while trying to board crowded trains. Taxi drivers may ignore a foreigner who is trying to hail a cab. The tendency to be slow and deliberate in making decisions is sometimes looked on as a sign of inconsideration, indecisiveness, or ineptitude by foreigners accustomed to the ''Do it now'' philosophy of the West. A young Japanese woman may respond to a question with nothing more than an embarrassed giggle, causing confusion and frustration for the Westerner who needs an answer.

When a foreigner is with a Japanese friend who runs into an acquaintance on the street, the foreigner may think it rude that his friend does not introduce him to his acquaintance. The friend, however, according to Japanese custom, sees no reason to make an introduction unless there is some practical reason for it; for example, if his acquaintance is in the same business as his foreign friend and the two may find a relationship mutually beneficial, then he may feel it appropriate to introduce them. If there is no specific purpose in an introduction, however, it will likely be left undone.

Women accustomed to the equal and often preferential treatment they receive in most Western countries may be offended by the appearance of male domination in Japan. (*See* "Gender Roles.") Particularly women on business or women who accompany their husbands on business in Japan are often frustrated that they are not considered or included in all cases as men are. They may also be offended that Japanese women themselves apparently accept their subordinate role so readily.

It is important to realize that customs can be "different" without necessarily being either superior or inferior to our own, so as to avoid either being offended or giving offense unnecessarily.

Phrases that can help you out of difficult situations include the following:

Dōmo sumimasen. Please excuse me.

Shitsurei shimashita. I was rude.

Daijōbu desu. / Ii desu yo. It's okay.

63. POPULATION

The population of Japan is 124,500,000 (1993)—approximately half that of the United States. The land area is about the size of Montana or two-thirds the size of California. Seventy-five percent of the land is mountainous and uninhabitable. Most of the population is clustered in and around major cities because of the highly centralized system of government and business.

64. PRIVACY

The Japanese concept of privacy does not have the same emphasis on individual rights as in the West. In Japan, privacy rights are often given over for what is deemed to be the welfare of the group or society in general. It is said that a term for "privacy rights" had to be coined in Japan when the Western legal concept was introduced following the Meiji Restoration in the 1860s.

As recently as fifty years ago, homes in Japan were built with an openness beyond what is customary in the West. Rooms were accessed via paper-paneled sliding doors without locks, and the concept of "my" and "your" within a family were subordinated to the greater importance of "our."

Today as well, even schools and companies cultivate a group ethic that overrides personal desires or ambitions. Administrators are parent figures, and they often know far more about their underlings' personal lives than do their counterparts in the West.

65. READING MATERIAL

The Japanese are avid readers, as witnessed by the large number of publications available at bookstores, kiosks, and newsstands. Major hotel bookstores usually offer a good selection of books in English and other languages for visitors. Four major English daily newspapers are published in Japan—*Japan Times, Mainichi Daily News, Daily Yomiuri*, and *Asahi Evening News*. There is also the *Nikkei Weekly*, which is similar in content to the *Wall Street Journal*. Since the Japanese spend a good deal of time on trains and buses, they often carry reading matter with them to occupy their time in transit. Visitors can also keep up with world news by way of CNN and other bilingual TV programs, as well as via radio over the Far East Network (FEN) of the U.S. Armed Forces Radio and Televison Service.

A relatively recent phenomenon, which gained great popularity in the 1960s, is the **manga** (comic book). Although some **manga** are similar to Western comic books, the Japanese take the concept much further to appeal to all ages and types of people, and **manga** have a function in all facets of life, from purely entertainment-type comics to informational comics and **manga**-style training supplements for businesses. Of growing concern is the large number of comics with sexually explicit or violently graphic themes. Although bookstores are encouraged to avoid selling such **manga** to children, the books are widely and easily available, even from vending machines in public places.

66. RELIGION

The distinction between religion and philosophy in Japan is blurred, and most Japanese do not adhere to one particular sect. The native religion is a mixture of **Shintō** (literally, "the way of the gods") and **Bukkyō** (Buddhism). There is no Sabbath (although Sunday is generally a day off from business, conforming to the Western standard), and there are no regularly scheduled worship meetings. Instead, people go to a shrine or temple at the beginning of the year and at other special times to pray and ask for blessings. Students preparing for entrance exams may pray for success by buying colorful wooden prayerboards called **ema**. Before starting the construction of a building, a Shinto priest may be called to offer prayers to appease the gods and spirits of the area.

Funerals are usually performed according to Buddhist rituals, and attendees burn incense for the dead at special altars. Weddings are commonly held according to Shinto rites or—a popular choice in recent years—western Christian style, with the bride in a white gown and the groom donning a tuxedo, even if neither the bride nor the groom is a follower of Christianity.

Shintō, a purely Japanese religion, is a loosely organized recognition of multiple **kami** (gods or spirits). Forces in nature— certain trees, rivers, mountains—are revered as places and things where such **kami** reside. Deceased relatives are also revered, and many families pay them homage at small altars in the home. Although Japan has no national religion today, Shinto was held as such until 1945. All Imperial Household rites, such as weddings, funerals, and ceremonies in conjunction with succession to the throne, are held according to Shinto tradition. Shinto emphasizes good behavior and harmonious relationships with people, nature, and spirits.

Bukkyō came from India by way of China and Korea and has undergone considerable alteration since its introduction to Japan in the year 538. There are now numerous sects whose differences primarily deal with specifics on how to obtain "nirvana," or salvation.

Taoism and **Confucianism** were also introduced from China. Taoism is based on the principle that the individual and the universe are separate but unified through Tao ("the Way") and that one must live in simplicity and harmony with nature. Its founder is the legendary figure Lao-Tse (372 to 289 B.C.). The teachings of the Chinese philosopher Confucius (551 to 479 B.C.) are based on social harmony and interpersonal relationships. Confucianism is considered the intellectual force behind the unification and stabilization of Japan as a nation under the Tokugawa family and had a great impact on Japanese thought and behavior.

Christianity was first introduced into Japan in 1549 by Jesuit missionaries from Portugal. They quickly found favor with local **daimyō** (feudal lords) in southwestern Japan, but although the church gained some popularity, it came to be viewed as a threat by the Tokugawa **Shōgun** (generalissimo), who feared the growing influence of Christianity against his authority, as well as the potential threat of military interference from Portugal and Spain. Christianity was banned, and a period of severe persecution followed until the Meiji Restoration. It was then reintroduced and has grown at a slow but fairly steady rate since World War II.

67. THE SEASONS

The four main islands of Japan are arranged in a bow shape from the northeast to the southwest, roughly comparable in both latitude and seasonal characteristics to the stretch from Maine to Georgia in the eastern United States.

Haru (spring) begins with the first pink blossoms of the plum tree, and is a time of both exhilaration and contemplation for the Japanese. As the weather warms, picnics and **hanami** (flower viewing) are enjoyed, as well as the composition of **haiku** (short, image-rich poems). This is also the time of **Golden Week**, when several national holidays fall within about a ten-day period. (*See* "Holidays and Festivals.")

Natsu (summer) brings heat and humidity, as well as considerable rainfall. The rainy season, called **tsuyu,** usually runs from mid-June to mid-July with continually cloudy skies and off-and-on drizzles. Farmers plant rice just before the expected beginning of **tsuyu,** and school vacations begin just as the rainy season is ending. The balance of the summer sees an increase in family vacation travel, beach and mountain visits, and other hot-weather activities, although the **taifū** (typhoon) season coincides with this period (August through September).

Aki (autumn) is beautiful in Japan, when the mountainous areas that comprise a major part of the country's geography are colored by **momiji** (changing colors of the leaves). Two areas especially noted for fall colors are Arashiyama in the Kyoto area and Aomori Prefecture, along the Oirase River.

Fuyu (winter) in the north is long and cold, and ice sculpture and other winter activities are enjoyed. Snow skiing is a popular sport, especially among young people. The southwest, however, enjoys very mild winters, suitable for their staple citrus fruits and other crops.

❁

68. SHOPPING

Japanese stores may be manned by many clerks, but customers are usually left alone to browse. Clerks do not approach until they are needed or requested to do so, and the commission system that is common in the West is not practiced in Japan.

Purchases are carefully—often artistically—wrapped in paper and sealed with tape. They also may be placed in a paper bag with the store's name and logo. The customer often goes home with a great deal more paper and plastic than might be considered necessary, a practice that is currently receiving some criticism from today's more environmentally conscious citizens.

Prices are clearly marked in most stores, and haggling and dickering are not common practices. Clerks do not count out change as is customary in the West, but customers are expected to do their own calculating while the transaction is being figured, to confirm the arithmetic. Cheating or taking advantage of customers rarely occurs in Japan. Any discrepancies or inconsistencies in a bill should, of course, be taken up with the clerk or manager and are generally the result of either an error on the part of the clerk or a misunderstanding on the part of the customer—or both.

Credit cards can be used at major hotels and some restaurants in Japan. As in the West, acceptable credit cards are displayed near the cash register. Traveler's checks are not as widely accepted, and it is advisable to exchange them for Japanese currency at a bank, using a passport as identification. Major banks have a designated foreign exchange (**ryōgae**) section marked in English.

Major hotel arcades offer convenient shopping for tourists, at premium prices. Department stores and specialty stores, however, are one way to experience the everyday life-style of the Japanese.

While department stores (**depāto**) dominate the large downtown areas, **shōtengai** (marketplaces) are still *the* place to shop in local neighborhoods. These collections of specialty shops are often situated in a pedestrians-only area—a block or more, often with a covering over the street to protect shoppers as they wander in and out of the various shops. Shop owners organize and share expenses for promotional investments, such as seasonal decorations and maintenance.

Supermarkets (**sūpā**) are relatively new to Japan and have gained considerable popularity, although many people still like to shop daily for fresh produce.

In some large metropolitan areas, certain hours on specific days are set aside for **Hokōsha Tengoku** (Pedestrian Paradise), when streets are limited to pedestrian traffic for several blocks to encourage and facilitate shopping.

69. SHRINES AND TEMPLES

Shinto shrines (**jinja** or **o-miya**) and Buddhist temples (**jiin** or **o-tera**) are considerably different in function from worship structures built by most Western churches. Although they are not used for regular worship gatherings, shrines and temples have year-round visitors, including those who look for spiritual fulfillment, students on educational and historical field trips, as well as tourists and others who appreciate the nation's culture.

Jinja are indicated on maps by the **torii** (gate) symbol, and Buddhist temples are marked with a **manji** symbol, which is similar to a swastika, but with the spokes turned in the opposite direction.

冂　　　卍

Visitors who wish to attend their own places of worship can find information in English-language newspapers available in most metropolitan areas.

70. SIGNATURES AND SEALS

As the credit card system slowly makes its way into Japan, personal signatures may become as widely accepted as they are in the West. Common practice today, however, is to use a personal seal-stamp called **han, hanko, inkan**, or **jitsuin**, which carries the person's surname and is used as a legal signature-stamp for all official documents. **Jitsuin** are registered at the local government office and used to validate important transactions.

Inexpensive **inkan** for everyday use can be found ready-made in stationery stores for common family names. Specialty shops deal in more personalized **han** carved on the patron's choice of wood, ivory, semiprecious stones, or other material.

Foreigners who would like to order personal **han** should first "Japanize" their names—either by transliteration (using the phonetic **katakana** characters) or by translation of the foreign name into an appropriate Japanese equivalent. For example, a Mr. Rivers might order a stamp that says リバース (**Ribāsu** in katakana, or one that says 河　 (**Kawa** "river" or "rivers", in kanji). Someone with the last name "Smith" might select either スミス (**Sumisu**) or 住巣　 (**Sumi-su**, "residence - nest"). Translations such as these are fun, but for business and any official or legal purposes, the foreigner's own legal name and signature should be used.

71. SOCIAL STRUCTURE

Japan's social structure, although there are no official designations or segregation, maintains a strong traditional influence based on both Buddhist and Confucian principles. Confucianism stresses that social harmony can exist only if proper relationships are maintained; that is, a person must be obedient to superiors and benevolent toward inferiors. The concepts of "superior" and "inferior" were based on five relational pairs: ruler/subject, father/son, husband/wife, elder/younger, and friend/friend.

Until the middle of the nineteenth century, there were four castes or classes of people. At the top were the **samurai** (warriors), followed in descending order by farmers (recognized as those who fed the nation), artisans (esteemed for their manual skills), and merchants (at the bottom of the social ladder because of their preoccupation with making money). By the end of the Tokugawa Period (1600 to 1868), the merchant class had gained much influence because they had become, as a whole, richer than the warrior class. Although they were nominally the lowest of the recognized classes, they held great power in the government of the country.

Above the **samurai** in name and reverence was the aristocracy, including the court and the Imperial Household and administrators, although the actual governance was, for most of Japan's history, left to the **samurai**.

An outcaste group included primarily those who dealt with blood, death, or filth, such as gravediggers, butchers, leatherworkers, and those who cleaned up after the classed citizens. Their unclean status stemmed from Buddhist taboos against such things as handling blood or eating or touching meat (other than fish or poultry). These outcastes were for centuries segregated from society, but today they possess all the legal rights of Japanese citizens, although they are still privately discriminated against by some individuals. Despite a growing movement against such prejudice, some families still hire "marriage detectives" to check out a person's ancestry before allowing a son or daughter to run the risk of being wed to someone of outcaste parentage.

72. SPORTS

Many Japanese are avid sports fans and both Western and traditional sports are popular. Baseball (**yakyū** or **beisubōru**) has been the favorite sport for many years and is known as the "national sport." In recent years, however, soccer (**sakkā**) has become extremely popular, especially among the young. Tennis and skiing have also gained wide appeal among the young and the elite, and golf is the sport of choice for businessmen.

Major universities have a long history of intercollegiate competition in rugby (**ragubii**), baseball, rowing (**bōto**), and soccer. Some companies sponsor Olympic-level volleyball teams, table tennis players, and others. American football was introduced into Japan following World War II, but it has not gained any particular following.

Many city dwellers have taken up jogging (**jogingu** or **marason**), aerobics (**erobikusu**), and swimming (**suiei**) as routine exercises and enjoy hiking (**haikingu**) and cycling (**saikuringu**) on weekends. The game most popular among senior citizens is a modified game of croquet called **geito-bōru** (gate-ball).

For individual sports, expenses are limited only by what the participant is willing to pay, with most Japanese placing much emphasis on having the best quality brand-name equipment, as well as professional lessons and, if possible, club memberships. Golf club memberships can run into the millions of dollars, making them well beyond the reach of the average person. Large companies often sponsor memberships for selected administrative personnel, however, and in recent years less expensive putting greens and driving ranges have sprung up in various places, providing opportunities for others to get a taste of the sport. Some companies also provide gymnasiums and exercise instructors for their employees, while tennis courts, batting ranges, and other sports facilities can be seen on the roofs of many company buildings.

Among traditional Japanese sports, **sumō** wrestling is the most popular and was the well-known favorite of the late Emperor Showa. Other popular sports include **kendō** (fencing with bamboo swords), **jūdō**, and other martial arts, as well as **kyūdō** (Japanese-style archery).

73. TABLE ETIQUETTE

Utensils should not be picked up until the host has prompted (**Go-enryo naku**—Please don't hesitate—or **Dōzo**—Go ahead). Before eating, it is customary to say, **Itadakimasu** (I shall partake). When the meal is over and the utensil is replaced on the table, the standard phrase to express appreciation is **Go-chisō-sama (deshita)** (Thank you for the feast).

It is considered bad manners to play, gesture, or point with chopsticks, to lick them, or to leave them sticking up in the rice or other food (a custom associated with funerals). It is also unacceptable to pass food from your chopsticks to someone else's or to serve yourself from a common bowl using the chopsticks you have been eating with. If separate serving utensils (**o-toribashi**) are not available, turn your own chopsticks around and use the clean ends to pick up food from a common dish.

When using **waribashi** (disposable "break-apart" chopsticks), people sometimes rub the two sticks together to remove any splinters or dip them into a glass of water to keep food from sticking to them, but both of these practices are considered tasteless and discourteous.

74. TELEPHONES

Most private homes in Japan have telephones, although installation costs are much higher than in the West. Public phones are widely available, and most accept both coins and magnetic telephone cards (**terehon kādo**), which are available at many stores and vending machines in denominations of　500,　1,000, and　3,000. For English-language information, dial one of the following numbers:

Tokyo	**3502–1461**
Kyoto	**371–5649**
elsewhere	**106**

Most Japanese public phones are green, except for those designated for international calling, which are grey. An international operator is accessed by dialing **0051**. Overseas calls originating in Japan are more expensive than incoming calls from other countries. It is economical to prearrange to receive calls when possible, or to use E-mail or fax.

In many stores, restaurants, and other businesses that have areas open to the public, there are pink phones that are specifically for local calls, and they accept only coins.

The Japanese equivalent of 911 emergency service is **110 (hyaku-tō-ban)**, and fire or ambulance service is accessed by dialing **119 (hyaku-jū-kyū-ban)**.

75. TELEVISION/RADIO/MOVIES

News and other TV and radio programs in English and some other languages are available in Japan. Offerings are listed in English-language newspapers. (*See* "Reading Material.") Included are CNN international programming, radio from the Far East Network (FEN) of the U.S. Armed Forces Radio and Television Services, and educational programming from NHK (**Nippon Hōsō Kyōkai**), the national broadcasting company.

Japanese TV series are limited to a certain number of episodes, similar to miniseries in the United States. Most series are 6-, 12-, or 24-weeks, although some recent historical dramas have lasted as long as a year. If a series is popular, it may be brought back with a slightly different name (as in the series "Tokyo Housewives," "Substitute Wives," and "Parliamentary Wives") or with "II" after its title ("Hotel" was followed by "Hotel II").

The quality of current TV programs is high. Foreign visitors will, however, notice some differences in both style and standards, compared with similar programming in the West. Game shows and soap operas are popular, along with music and variety programs and drama series. The quality and unique character of Japanese **anime** (animated movies) have in recent years created a cult following in the United States and other countries. **Anime** are available both on TV and in movie theaters, as well as in video format for rent or purchase.

Foreign movies are popular in Japan, particularly offerings from the United States. The visitor should be aware, however, that foreign movies may be dubbed for the benefit of the Japanese viewer, rather than subtitled.

Foreigners who live in Japan for any length of time may purchase an attachment for the television that provides for bilingual broadcasting (**nika kokugo hōsō**), allowing the viewer to hear certain programs in English or other languages. Daily newspapers include listings of available bilingual programming.

✿

76. THANK-YOUS AND REGRETS

The Japanese language is rich with special ways to express gratitude and regret. Although **Dōmo arigatō gozaimasu** is a standard "thank-you," some particular situations call for more customized phrases, including the following;

O-machidō-sama deshita.	Thank you for waiting.
Go-chisō-sama deshita.	Thank you for the meal.
Go-kurō-sama deshita.	Thank you for going out of your way. (This phrase is appropriate for expressing thanks to peers or underlings, but not to superiors.)
O-tsukare-sama deshita.	Thank you for your hard work. (This also is more appropriate for peers and underlings, although it was originally used exclusively among stage performers without regard to age or standing.)

Similarly, apologies are expressed in various ways, the most common being **Gomen nasai** and **Sumimasen**, both of which translate as "I'm sorry" or "Excuse me." Some other expressions of apology or regret include the following:

Shitsurei itashimashita.	Forgive me for being rude.
O-saki ni shitsurei itashimasu.	Excuse me for going ahead of you.
Gomen nasai.	Please forgive me./I'm sorry.

In casual situations both thank-yous and apologies are often shortened or otherwise made less formal; for example, **Dōmo** is an acceptable casual expression of gratitude, and **itashimasu** or **itashimashita** is often replaced by the less formal **shimasu** or **shimashita**.

77. THEATER

Dramatic arts have been an important part of Japanese culture since at least the 14th century, with the introduction of **Nō**, the highly stylized, one-act classic drama using male actors. The **Nō** production is simple—its slow, deliberate movements presented on a bare stage to flute and drum accompaniment, with masked actors and a chorus chanting the story-verse as the dance is performed.

The more popular **Kabuki** theater form combines stylized acting, elaborate staging and costumes, as well as special theatrical effects, including trap doors and elevators, curtains, revolving stages, and quick changes of costume. Attendance at a **Kabuki** performance is normally an hours-long affair, but many city tours include a short visit to the theater to view an hour or so of the performance.

Bunraku is traditional Japanese puppet theater and is geared toward adults, rather than children. **Bunraku** puppets are exquisitely carved figures as much as four feet in height and so highly mobile that even movements of the fingers, lips, eyes, and eyebrows can be accomplished with realistic fluidity, requiring as many as three puppeteers to manipulate each figure.

Although **Nō** and **Bunraku** are patronized only by true

theater lovers, **Kabuki** is far more popular and is considered by many to be a mandatory experience for the true Japanophile.

78. TIME AND PUNCTUALITY

Tokyo time is 17 hours ahead of Los Angeles, California. That is, if it is noon on Wednesday in Los Angeles, it is 5 A.M. Thursday in Tokyo. As in the United States, the Japanese use the 12-hour clock for the most part, with the military, railroads, and some others using the 24-hour clock. Daylight saving time is not observed.

The Japanese, particularly those who live or work in metropolitan areas, are very time-conscious and punctual. Trains, buses, and planes run on an exacting schedule; business meetings begin punctually; and clocks in public places are well maintained and synchronized.

79. TIPPING AND SERVICE CHARGES

There is no custom of tipping in Japan, and clerks, waitresses, cab drivers, and others who may be offered a gratuity by a foreign patron will usually refuse it. However, hotels and inns automatically place service charges on bills. When a restaurant bill exceeds a certain amount, a service charge is assessed and included in the total.

80. TOILETS

The standard style of commode in Japan is a porcelain fixture similar in shape to a men's urinal, but installed in the floor. (Urinals are also available in public men's rooms.) Western-style toilets (the sit-down type) can be found in many public facilities, large downtown stores and restaurants, and in some homes, although the floor model is preferred by many families. In public facilities it is not uncommon to find an instructional chart on the wall next to a Western-style toilet, indicating with stick-figures how it should be used.

It is common for small establishments to have one tiny restroom with a urinal and a Japanese-style commode for both men and women's use. It is best to knock to see that it is not in use, since people often forget to lock the doors.

When looking for a restroom, ask for the **toire** or **otearai**, not the **o-furo** or **furoba** (bathroom),which is a room that has a bathtub but usually no toilet. Since Japanese public restrooms do not ordinarily supply paper towels, most Japanese carry a cloth handkerchief for drying the hands after washing. These handkerchiefs are *not* used to blow the nose. For that purpose, tissue (**chirigami**) is carried instead.

81. TRAVEL WITHIN JAPAN

Japanese bus, train, and air service is convenient, efficient, and reliable. A traveler with a reasonable understanding of Japanese spoken and written language can get around in Japan with relative ease. If your Japanese is minimal, however, it is advisable to take a friend or travel with a group. Numerous tours leave daily for various destinations and are accessible via your hotel desk or a local travel service. Travel services and agencies are abundant in Japan, the largest of these being the Japan Travel Bureau (JTB).

The **Shinkansen**, known internationally as the "Bullet Train," is a high-speed rail line that links Tokyo with Kyushu in the southwest, Niigata on the Japan Sea, and Morioka at the northern tip of the main island of Honshu.

The mass transit systems of Tokyo and other metropolitan areas of Japan are among the best, most reliable, most punctual, and safest in the world. Far more commuters choose rail and bus transportation over private cars for daily travel needs.

Signs indicating train stops and station names are written in the

Roman alphabet, as well as in Japanese script, which makes it possible for even non-Japanese-speaking visitors to find their way around town with relative independence. Rail lines are color-coded to help passengers identify trains and stations. Maps, which are widely available, are made easier to read by the color coordination.

Large wall charts of the various rail lines can be found at any train or subway station (**eki**) near the **kaisatsu-guchi** (ticket gates) and ticket vending machines. In major stations these charts may include Romanized versions of station names; otherwise, there is always someone around who will be willing to help foreign visitors locate the station of their destination, purchase a **kippu** (ticket) at the automatic vending machines, find their way to the appropriate **hōmu** (platform), and point out the place where they need to transfer (**norikae**).

Chikatetsu (subway)   Subway facilities are clean, well lighted, and colorful. Vandalism and crime are rare problems. Subway lines connect at various points with other train lines and run on frequent schedules.

Densha (electric train)   Surface trains are the choice for areas where the subway does not reach. In Tokyo the **Yamanote-sen** (Yamanote line) runs in a large loop around the metropolis, connecting at numerous points with other surface and subway lines.

Basu (buses)   Buses are also clean, convenient, punctual, and frequent. Bus **noriba** (boarding places) are well marked, with arrival times posted at each stop. Even though the signs are written for the Japanese reader, times are written in Arabic numerals, making it possible for others to decipher needed information.

Takushii (taxis)   The best places to get a cab are the **takushii noriba** (taxi stands) at all railway stations and in front of hotels (where bellhops can assist). Taxis are privately owned, are available in all metropolitan areas, and can be hired for more distant travel, if the passenger is willing to pay the price. Taxi drivers know major landmarks and train stations but may have difficulty finding stores or residences because of the Japanese house numbering system. (*See* "Addresses and Street Names.")

If you have an appointment, however, it is often better to go by public transit, rather than taxi. Although it is illegal, many taxi drivers pick and choose their fares. It is also illegal for a taxi driver to charge more than the usual rate during late hours, but this, too, happens on occasion. Visitors are advised to do their traveling during the hours when train and bus lines are running. A good phrase to remember is **Densha** (or **Basu**) **wa nanji made desu ka?** (How late does the train/bus run?) Business travelers may have company cars and drivers available to them for official travel.

Another important item to keep in mind is that Japanese taxis have doors that operate automatically. *Never* try to open or close a taxi door yourself.

82. VENDING MACHINES

Vending machines (**jidōhanbaiki**) in Japan are ubiquitous, generally well maintained, and rarely vandalized. They offer a much greater variety of goods than in the West, including both fresh and packaged foods and drinks, reading material, personal grooming items, items of clothing, and more. Many items that are not allowed in public vending machines in the United States are available via **jidōhanbaiki** in Japan—tobacco, alcohol, pornographic publications, and condoms, for example.

83. VISITING PRIVATE HOMES

The Japanese do not ordinarily entertain people in their own homes, but prefer to use restaurants or hotels instead. However, a recent trend is to have **gaikokujin** or **gaijin** (foreigners) visit their homes. Foreign visitors should take a supply of hometown products for such occasions, preferably a midrange or relatively sophisticated gift, as opposed to a cheap token souvenir. Gift boxes of food or craft products are appropriate. For subsequent visits a smaller gift of cut flowers, sweets, or fruits purchased locally are acceptable.

Needless to say, dropping by someone's home unannounced is not commonly done, except perhaps for young people or couples who are close friends and live near one another. Even relatives outside the immediate family will ordinarily telephone first.

In the case of a formal home visit, the visitor should remove hat, coat, and scarf and carry them over an arm before ringing the doorbell. In inclement weather, listen for footsteps from inside the house before removing the coat.

In the **genkan** (entryway) shoes are removed, and the host presents slippers for the visitors. (*See* "Footwear.") The American custom of taking a tour of the house is not practiced in Japan. Visitors are entertained in the **ribingu** (living room).

When invited for lunch, the visitor usually leaves by 3:00, at the latest. For an evening meal, visitors do not stay any later than 8:00 P.M. Even when the host urges a guest to stay, it is expected that the visitor will insist on leaving anyway, however reluctantly. The host and family will then see the visitor off at the door or, if possible, go with the visitor as far as the transit station.

If leave-taking is done at the door, the entire family will come to the entryway, the lady of the house kneeling while the guest changes into street shoes, and the others help the visitor with coat and other belongings. Some of the family members will wave and bow from the doorway, while others accompany the guest to the gate or to the car. The guest will turn around at least once and bow or wave before getting into the car and heading off down the street.

In many cases the host or a member of the family will see the visitor to the station, either by car or on foot, and may even buy the visitor's ticket. The person will then stand at the station entrance and wait until the visitor is out of sight before returning home. Again, the visitor will turn around at least once and bow to the host before disappearing into the station.

It is important that the visitor remember to express gratitude to the host when they meet for the first time following the visit. A good phrase to remember is **Kinō wa** (or **Senjitsu wa**) **dōmo arigatō gozai-mashita.** (Thank you very much for yesterday/the other day.)

84. WEIGHTS, MEASURES, AND SIZES

The Metric System   Since Japan uses the metric system of measurement, visitors unaccustomed to that system would do well to carry a conversion chart. Following are some basic comparisons between the U.S. customary system and the metric system:

1 centimeter = 0.4 inch	1 inch = 2.5 centimeters
1 meter = 39.3 inches	1 foot = .305 meter
1 kilometer = 0.625 mile	1 mile = 1.6 kilometers
1 liter = 1.06 quarts	1 quart = .95 liter
1 gram = .035 ounces	1 ounce = 28.35 grams
1 kilogram = 2.2 pounds	1 pound = .454 kilograms

Temperature   Japan measures temperature by the Celsius (Centigrade) gauge. To convert from Celsius to Fahrenheit degrees, multiply by 9/5 and add 32; to convert from Fahrenheit to Centrigrade, subtract 32 and then multiply the remainder by 5/9. Following are some basic comparisons.

Freezing point of water = 0°C or 32°F
Mild spring weather = 20°C or 68°F
Normal body temperature = 37°C or 98.6°F
Boiling point of water = 100°C or 212°F

Clothing Sizes   Clothing sizes in Japan are often simply "S" for "small," "M" for "medium," "L" for "large," and "LL" for "extra-large." It should be kept in mind that these relative sizes are smaller than the Western concept of "small," "medium," and "large," since average Japanese physical stature is generally smaller and shorter than the average for a Westerner. Proportions are different, also, and long-limbed Americans should not expect to dress themselves "off the rack" in Japan.

Metric sizes are used for shoes, shirts, and some other items; for example, someone who buys a size 7 shoe in the United States will look for a size 24½ in Japan, and an American shirt collar size of 15 translates to about a 38 in Japanese sizes. Dress shoes over size 7½ are hard to find and may cost over $200 a pair. Very narrow ("A"–"AAA") widths are also rare.

85. WORKING HOURS

Basic business hours in Japan are 9-to-5, as in the West, but the flextime system is encouraged to ease rush-hour problems in public transit. Also, many white-collar employees put in long hours each day, usually without additional compensation, invariably arriving at work 5 to 10 minutes before starting time and staying until the supervisor leaves. Stores and other small businesses also keep hours comparable to similar establishments elsewhere, including convenience stores (**konbini**) and many small, family-type stores, especially those near train stations, that are open late.

The workweek is usually Monday through Friday for offices; however, smaller stores and businesses are open Saturdays; some are open Sundays as well; and many public schools hold a short day of classes on Saturday morning and close altogether on one Saturday each month. Vacation time is available to employees, similar to Western standards, although white-collar workers rarely take more than a few days at a time for vacation, and sick leave is taken only for real illnesses.

Good phrases to remember include the following:

Teikyūbi wa itsu desu ka? What day of the week is your store closed?

Yasumi desu ka? Are you closed?

86. THE WRITTEN LANGUAGE

The Japanese written characters are adapted from the Chinese writing system and consist of three different sets of characters.

Kanji are ideographs and pictographs similar to the Chinese characters, but with some modifications for simplicity. Each individual **kanji** carries a particular meaning, but may be pronounced several different ways, depending on the way it is used.

Katakana is a phonetic system of 46 characters used for words of foreign origin, to call attention to a word, or for some other specific purposes. It is used extensively in advertising. Each character represents a syllable of sound—usually either a vowel sound alone or a consonant-and-vowel combination. There is no inherent meaning in any character.

Hiragana is also a phonetic system, representing the same 46 syllables as **katakana,** but it is used to write verb endings, for grammatical words such as particles and conjunctions, and for any word for which there is no designated **kanji.**

Katakana and **hiragana** are collectively called **kana.** The two **kana** systems can be used to write anything in the Japanese language, but because of the large number of words that sound alike but have different meanings, **kanji** is necessary to clarify meaning. Attempts have been made to promote the use of **kana** or **rōmaji** (the Roman alphabet) exclusively, but such attempts have not gained much popular support, because of inherent and obvious logistical problems.

Schoolchildren learn **kana** by the end of the first year of school (most learn at least **hiragana** at home or in preschool), along with some **kanji.** More **kanji** are added to the curriculum each year through high school, up to a total of approximately 1850 **kanji.** The Ministry of Education determines which **kanji** are taught each year in the public schools.

漢字　　カタカナ　　ひらがな

87. "YES" AND "NO"

Generally speaking, the Japanese feel that saying ''no'' is too abrupt a response for most situations, both business and personal, and that it can eliminate the possibility of negotiation. Instead of saying ''no,'' a slight cocking of the head while audibly inhaling or exhaling air is understood by the Japanese to mean that something is very difficult or impossible. This may be accompanied by **Chotto . . .** or one of the phrases shown below:

This is a little difficult.	**Chotto muzukashii desu.**
I really don't know.	**Chotto wakarimasen.**
I understand what you are saying, but. . .	**Ossharu koto wa wakari- masu ga. . .**
I wonder if it can be done.	**Sā, dekimasu deshō ka.**
I will give it a try, but. . .	**Doryoku shimasu ga. . .**
Let me discuss it with others.	**Sōdan shite mimasu.**
Let me have some time.	**Sukoshi jikan o kudasai.**
Let me think about it.	**Kangaesasete kudasai.**

A point of confusion for many newcomers to Japan is the Japanese response to a negative question. When a question is posed in a negative form, as in *"Won't* you have something to drink?" or *"Don't* you understand?"*, it is answered as if it were a true-false question; for example, in response to the question **O-cha o nomimasen ka** (Won't you have some tea?/Don't you drink tea?), a person may say **Hai, ima kekkō desu** (Yes/true, I don't care for any right now). If a response to the question **Wakarimasen ka** (Do you *not* understand?) is **Hai**, the meaning is "Yes/true, I do not understand"; if the response is **Iie**, the intended meaning is "No/false, I *do* understand."

Another source of misunderstanding is the Japanese habit of using **hai** or **ee** simply to acknowledge a question, even when the answer to the question itself is negative, as in the following exchange:

Q: **Nimotsu mada arimasu ka?** Do you have any more luggage?

A: **Ee, mō nain desu.** Yes (I understand your question), I don't have any more.

Q: **Mō arimasen ka?** There isn't any more?

A: **Ee.** Yes, (you are right).

A safeguard against misunderstanding for any newcomer to Japan would be to ask for a clarification to an unexpected response or to any response that is not clear, as in the example above. When giving an answer to a negative question, it is best to answer with a statement, rather than simply **hai** or **iie**.

Q: **Wakarimasen ka?** Don't you understand?

A: **(Hai,) wakarimasen.** (Yes,) I don't understand *or* **(Iie,) wakarimasu** No, I do understand.

88. "YOU FIRST"

In contrast to the Western tradition of "ladies first," the Japanese tradition is "you first"; that is, for the sake of courtesy, the other person is placed on a higher social level than oneself. This is reflected in speech, in body language and "personal space" accommodation, in social forms and rituals of etiquette, and in many other aspects of Japanese life.

Guests, customers, clients, and visitors are generally given the first right of refusal on everything from going through a doorway to choice of food and drink. Polite phrases to remember include the following:

(O-saki ni) dōzo.	Please, (go ahead).
Go-enryo naku.	Don't hesitate.
Dōmo sumimasen.	Excuse me.
O-saki ni shitsurei shimasu.	I apologize for going ahead of you.

A seeming exception to the "you first" rule is that in a mixed group, going through a doorway, for example, men are expected to go first (lead by the senior male, if one is present), with women following. On a crowded train or bus, there is no social expectation for a man to give up his seat to a woman, no matter how many packages or children she may be carrying.

89. ZOOLOGICAL CALENDAR

The question "What's your sign?" may elicit a different immediate response in Japan than in the United States, as the Japanese give more consideration to the zoological sign for a birth year than the astrological sign of a birthday. It is also considered less direct to ask the zoological calendar year of a person's birth than to ask a person's age: **Nani doshi umare desu ka.** (In what [zoological] calender year were you born?) Adapted from the Chinese, the zoological calendar runs in a 12-year cycle, as follows:

Nezumi-doshi (Year of the Rat): 1924, 36, 48, 60, 72, 84, 96
Ushi-doshi (Year of the Ox): 1925, 37, 49, 61, 73, 85
Tora-doshi (Year of the Tiger): 1926, 38, 50, 62, 74, 86
Usagi-doshi (Year of the Hare): 1927, 39, 51, 63, 75, 87
Tatsu-doshi (Year of the Dragon): 1928, 40, 52, 64, 76, 88
Hebi-doshi (Year of the Snake): 1929, 41, 53, 65, 77, 89
Uma-doshi (Year of the Horse): 1930, 42, 54, 66, 78, 90
Hitsuji-doshi (Year of the Sheep): 1931, 43, 55, 67, 79, 91
Saru-doshi (Year of the Monkey): 1932, 44, 56, 68, 80, 92
Tori-doshi (Year of the Cock): 1933, 45, 57, 69, 81, 93
Inu-doshi (Year of the Dog): 1934, 46, 58, 70, 82, 94
Inoshishi-doshi (Year of the Boar): 1935, 47, 59, 71, 83, 95

SOURCES AND RELATED READINGS

All-Japan: the Catalogue of Everything Japanese. New York: Quill, 1984.

Bunce, William K. *Religions in Japan.* Rutland, Vermont: Charles E. Tuttle Co., 1955.

Chambers, Kevin. *Asian Customs & Manners.* New York: Meadowbrook (Simon & Schuster), 1988.

Danziger, Charles. *The American Who Couldn't Say Noh.* New York: Kodansha, 1994.

Hayashiya, Umesao and Tada Kato. *Nihonjin no Chie.* Tokyo: Chū ōkoron-sha, 1973.

Hoffer, B. and N. Honna. *An English Dictionary of Japanese Culture.* Tokyo: Yuhikaku Publishing Co., Ltd., 1986.

How Bridgestone Works. Tokyo: Bridgestone Co., Inc., 1994.

Japan. Alexandria, Virginia: Time-Life Books, 1986.

Japan: Profile of a Nation. Tokyo: Kodansha International, 1995.

Japan of Today, The. Tokyo: The International Society for Educational Information, Inc., 1993.

Kato, Hiroki and Joan Kato. *Understanding and Working with the Japanese Business World.* Englewood Cliffs, NJ: Prentice Hall, 1992.

Lampkin, Rita L. *Japanese Verbs & Essentials of Grammar.* Lincolnwood, Illinois: Passport Books, 1994.

Maloney, Don. *Japan: It's Not All Raw Fish.* Tokyo: The Japan Times, Ltd., 1975.

Mizutani, Osamu and Nobuko. *Nihongo Notes 1-4*. Tokyo: The Japan Times, 1981.

Nippon: Business Facts & Figures. 1993-94, Tokyo: Japan External Trade Organization (JETRO), 1993-94.

U.S. and Japan in Figures, I, II, III. 1991-1994, Tokyo: JETRO, 1991-94.

Morimoto, Tetsuro. *Nihongo Nehori Hahori*. Tokyo: Shincho-sha, 1991.

The New Grolier Multimedia Encyclopedia. Grolier, Inc., 1993.

Nihon Dai Hyakka Jiten (Encyclopedia Japan). Tokyo: Shogakukan, 1988.

Nishihara, Nomoto, et al. *Gaikokujin Bijinesu Kankeisha no Tame no Nihongo Kyōiku Q & A*. Tokyo: Bunkacho Kokugoka, 1994.

Nishihara, Nomoto, et al. *Ibunka Rikai no Tame no Nihongo Kyōiku Q & A*. Tokyo: Bunkacho Kokugoka, 1994.

Japan, a Business Traveler's Handbook. Tokyo: PHP Institute, 1990.

Tetsuzuki Handobukku 1995. Tokyo: Tosho Insatsu Co., Ltd., 1995.

Reischauer, Edwin O. *The Japanese*. Cambridge, MA: The Belknap Press of Harvard University Press, 1982.

Takada, N. and H. Kato. *Just Listen n' Learn Japanese*. Lincolnwood, IL: Passport Books (NTC Publishing Group), 1994.

Tazawa, Matsubara, and Okuda Nagahata. *Japan's Cultural History, A Perspective*. Tokyo: Ministry of Foreign Affairs, 1973.

Umesao, Tadao, ed. *Seventy-Seven Keys to the Civilization of Japan*. Osaka: Sogensha, Inc., 1985.

INDEX

A

A&W 21
abbreviations 1
acronyms 7
acupuncture 64
address, forms of 62
addresses 2, 55, 83
Adults' Day 42
affection 24, 57
agreement 14, 24, 65
Akihito, Emperor/Crown Prince 11, 44, 52
All-Souls' Festival 45
Amaterasu Ōmikami 51
animals 15, 61, 64
anime 77
Aomori 70
apologies 78
appreciating quality 9
appreciation 7, 23, 31, 37, 44, 51, 76
Arabic numerals 63
Arbor Day 42
arts 3, 12, 28, 31, 36, 51, 73, 79
asking directions 3
Autumnal Equinox 43

B

bamboo 32, 45, 75
banks 56, 59, 71
bathing 4, 48, 49
bathrooms 4, 34, 49
bathtubs 4, 33, 81
bean-throwing ritual 44
bed & breakfast 48
behavior 5, 16, 69
birthdays 42, 44, 45, 90
body language 6
bonsai 3, 31
bonuses 46
borrowed words 7, 45, 54
bowing 9, 15, 37
brand names 9, 55
Buddha's Birthday 45
Buddhism 17–18, 30, 31, 41, 45, 50, 68–69, 72, 74
Bullet Train 81
Bunraku 79
burial 17
buses 3, 67, 80, 81–82, 89
business 2, 6, 7–8, 10–11, 15, 22–25, 29–30, 36, 38, 52–56, 62, 66, 73, 86, 87
business cards 10–11, 62
business hours 86
businessmen 26, 55, 74
butsudan 41, 50

C

calendar 11–12, 32, 89–90
calligraphy 3
central heating 49
checking accounts 56, 59
cherry blossoms 12–13, 32

INDEX

INDEX

INDEX

White Day 39
women 5, 22, 25, 26, 36, 39, 53, 59,
    62, 66, 81, 89
workaholism 55
Workers' Day 45
working hours 86
World War II 2, 28, 30, 39, 43, 52, 55,
    70, 75
World's Fair 21
written language 76–77, 86–87

Y

Yakuza 15
year's end 46
yen 59
Yes and No 87–88
You First 89

Z

zoological calendar 89–90